The Hamlyn Book of
Garden Ideas

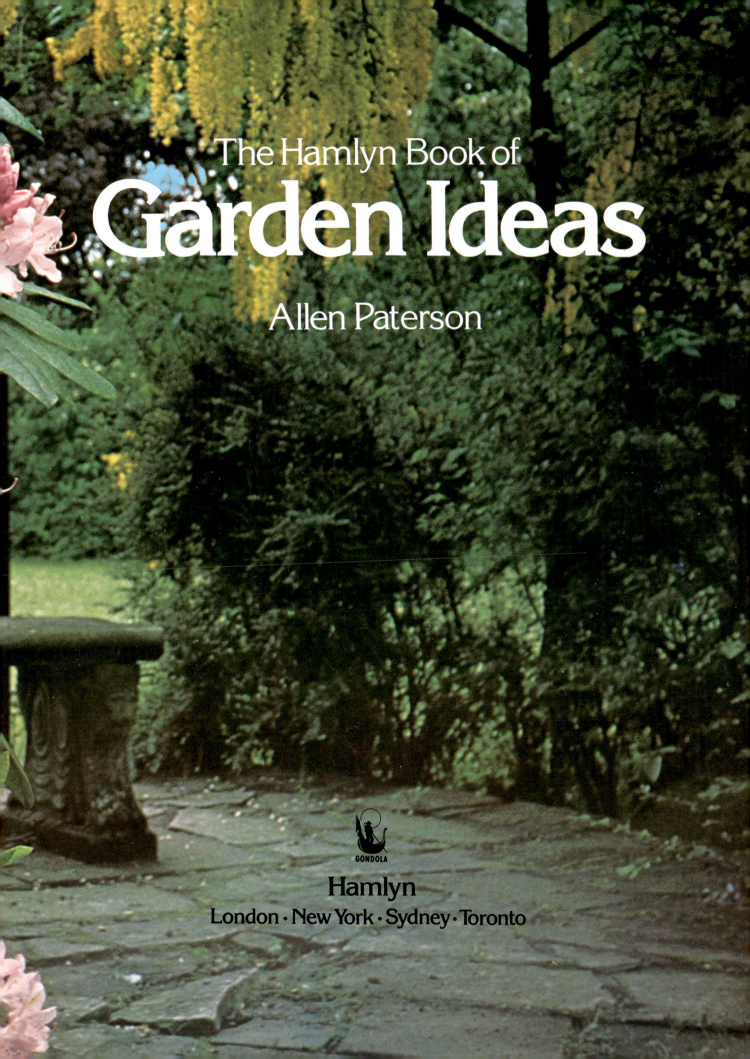

The Hamlyn Book of
Garden Ideas

Allen Paterson

GONDOLA

Hamlyn
London · New York · Sydney · Toronto

Contents

Foreword

For E.O.P. who is at least half responsible

WHY DOES ANYONE EVER WRITE A BOOK. THERE MUST BE MANY ostensible reasons. To 'Make a Name' perhaps, or because one has something to say which, it is egotistically thought, will be of interest, amusement or even practical help to other people. And, it should be stated at once, putative authors are lured by publishers' crocks of gold at the end of the rainbow. Except, of course, the road that is laboriously followed sometimes resembles more a slough of despond than the expected multicoloured path in the sky.

Yet, as it can be seen on every hand in every bookshop, there is no lack of people rashly exposing to critical gaze their wares: their thoughts on every subject under the sun. Why *do* they do it?

This particular field of books on gardening topics is especially vulnerable to such exposure. No doubt the authors' basic *raisons d'etre* are no more, nor less venal to those of other authors. But gardening writers are obvious butts. For everyone is a gardener and hence a critic with actual practical knowledge of the subject to call upon and to put against that which is on the printed page. Therefore everyone can offer something, and often something of value, to a discussion on gardens and gardening.

Hence yet another book on design for small gardens is foolhardy indeed if it purports to offer a great deal that is new. Hopefully what it does do is to restate in contemporary terms and for contemporary needs the problems which have exercised gardeners since Adam and Eve were forced to leave that first extremely agreeable garden which, apparently, needed no maintenance. The continuum of essays in this field is the bibliography of the history of gardening, an on-going process in our attempt to ameliorate our conditions and to improve our lives.

This book aims at encouraging thinking people to think about their gardens – basically about whether they are getting what they want from their plots. Alan Hart's plans are not meant to be slavishly copied – though they could be, because as designs they work – but to be used in association with the text as discussion material related to any particular plot.

No apology is made for basing much, though not all, of the material on a conventional rectangular strip, it is after all the fate of the majority of gardening pretensions. Nor is apology made for opening the conversation with the apparently grandiose thoughts of an early 18th century Augustan satirist. What Alexander Pope put into elegant stanzas still has sense to offer us, in spite of, not because of its being said so beautifully – though he might not have waxed so lyrical if confronted with a 20th-century back garden. But that is what we have: it does seem a pity not to make the most of it.

Part 1

Design
for Gardens

What Have You Got?

AT SOME TIME OR ANOTHER everyone notices a particular garden feature or an especially spectacular plant and says 'That's something I *must* have' or 'That I must grow when I have a garden of my own'. This is good; anyone who gardens for pleasure (and if much of it is not pleasure, one might might as well move into a flat at once) is inevitably sparked off by seeing and recognising success in gardens already made. They may be the local parks, a little front garden up the road, a seaside site seen on holiday or a great country-house garden visited.

Know Your Limitations
The most important thing in deciding how to make a new garden or how to improve an existing one (usually this is much the easier task) is to know what is feasible in the area in which you live. And there is no better way than seeing what groups of plants do well in your own area and what sort of garden features look right there. Because, however much one admires the marvellous rhododendrons at, shall we say, the Royal Horticultural Society's Gardens at Wisley, there is no point in trying to repeat the effect at home, if home is on a limy soil. They will just die. The most depressing garden I have ever seen was made at enormous expense in a beautiful valley in chalky downlands: a little stream had been widened and dammed, the sound of water gently falling over rocks making a charming effect, with wide shrub borders swelling and receding to follow the contours of the hills just as the treatises on design say it

should be done. *But*, all these borders were planted with mature rhododendrons and azaleas – splendid plants that must have cost a fortune – and all were yellowing and dying in evident agony with lumps of solid chalk mixed up with the peat that was supposed to help.

The point of this salutary story is that every garden must be improved within – as the famous Mr Brown would have said in the 18th century – its capabilities. The seaside holiday and the country-house garden offer ideas, themes and suggestions, not for slavish copying but for adaption to suit particular needs.

How then to start planning a garden? Capability Brown, I have always thought, made his famous and inevitable remark, 'It has capabilities, my Lord' when being shown the broad acres designated for landscape improvement, to play for time. While all the while really thinking 'Hell's teeth! What can I do with this?' Yet the effect – particularly from our perspective two centuries later – was invariably so masterly as to make Brown's landscapes appear perfect natural countryside or just what Nature would have done if she had had a tidier mind.

For what Brown did, and all really effective designers have done since, was to follow Pope's precepts. The lines are well-known:

'Consult the genius of the place in all
That tells the water or to rise, or fall,
Or helps the ambitious hill the heavens to scale,
Or scoops in circling theatres the vale,

Calls in the country, catches opening glades,
Joins willing woods, and varies shades from shades,
Now breaks, or now directs, the intending lines
Paints as you plant, and as you work designs.'

But does Brown, working in thousands of acres (hectares weren't thought of) with endless cheap labour, or does a dilettante poet-gardener like Alexander Pope have any relevance to us today? Does my back garden 6m by 9m (20ft by 30ft) possess a 'genius' at all? I believe it has. I think one has got to presume the existence (call it the 'distinctive character' to make it sound less archaic if you will) as the combination of inevitabilities to be worked with, not fought against in any garden of any size.

The Distinctive Character
This distinctive character will fight back and ultimately win, just as that chalk valley beat the rhododendrons that had no conceivable connection with it.

The character, then, is made up of the soil, the aspect, the climatic conditions of that particular part of the country, the views or lack of them, the buildings around, and so on. The combination may be so unpromising as to be difficult in the extreme, but no site is incapable of being improved by thoughtful design and carefully chosen plants well looked after.

The Importance of Plants
Only in the most esoteric of Japanese gardens do plants have no place and even there the inevitable

and insidious weathering of the all-important rocks causes a gradual accumulation of mosses and lichens. To the Western mind, however, a space deprived of all but the more primitive plants cannot deserve the title of garden. Gardens, we feel, are for plants and for people. Their very aliveness is part of their importance to us, however small they are.

This does not mean that the basic design of the simplest suburban strip is not just as important as in the bare, contemplative, oriental mode. It is; and in many ways it is vastly more difficult to plan for plant growth. For a garden is really a big, living, 3-D, walk-through sculpture. It is seen from a multitude of angles – though some sight lines are more important (from the kitchen windows for instance) than others – from above, from the end of the garden and from half way down.

The Initial Design
This should encompass those things that we want – within the confines of the site and the depth of our pocket. It will place and arrange flowers and shrubs, lawn and vegetable patch, fruit trees and bushes; it will site a sitting-out area to catch the sun and a compost heap to recycle all spare organic material. It will decide upon paths and drives and where the washing is to be hung out to dry.

These are the elements of design; the fitting together of the ultimate in jigsaw puzzles. A jigsaw which has unlimited pieces of varying shapes to make up the picture that is not yet on the front of the box. It sounds daunting, if not completely impossible.

So we return to the distinctive character of the place for it is that which will determine, in general, what sort of pieces each particular puzzle of a garden will contain, while the garden-maker more clearly controls their shape. Again, it must be repeated, we must work *with* what we have, not against it, if

anything approaching success is to be achieved. The shape of the design and the hard materials do what they are told; plants, with few exceptions, do what they must. That is, they grow to the best of their ability not to please the gardener but to try to reproduce their species. Perhaps it's as well that carrots cannot know that their fine accumulated foodstores end up in a stew instead of providing the energy to rocket up a flower spike the summer following that winter rest!

The Requirements of Plants
These must be considered if they are to be happy – and that to them is to be biologically successful – organisms filling the niche in the contrived walk-through sculpture we call a garden. Like animals, plants that we all normally cultivate, have specific needs to be able to live. These needs, simply, are fivefold: warmth, food, air, light, water, and wherever these factors combine, plant growth will happen; watch a piece of bare earth for a few months and see.

In the wild and even in neglected bare patches in gardens, if left alone, the plants which colonise the site will be just those that have adapted, over aeons, to succeed on just that soil in just that climate and in just that amount of shade. If they do not succeed then they are pushed out by those that can. Fortunately a cultivated plot is not quite so blatant an example of nature, green in thorn and spine as the plant world might be described. And we are able to ameliorate, if not change, the local conditions so that our plants represent a vastly greater environmental range than just that of our own wild flora. But we neglect the natural environment and plants' requirements at our peril.

Warmth
Of the five essentials the most likely to restrict plant growth in temperate

climes is warmth or, to be exact, lack of it. So clearly the part of the country in which one lives makes a great deal of difference. It is often said that Great Britain doesn't have a climate – only weather – and certainly in gardening the combination of small factors that make each garden's microclimate is vital.

In general the winter minimum temperatures commonly experienced are the most limiting factor governing any choice of plants. And in Great Britain these are most likely to be lower in the east whilst the west has milder winters. Hence the surprise in seeing fine palm-trees and tree-ferns in wind-sheltered gardens in the north-west of Scotland which would have no hope of succeeding in Kent, some 500 miles to the south.

It should also be remembered that temperature at the plant's roots is vital. A heavy clay soil holding large amounts of water will keep the temperature low in winter as well as being very slow to warm up in the vital early days of spring. Many desirable garden plants, especially from dry Mediterranean regions, such as lavenders, rosemary and rock roses find such a soil an unpleasant and unsatisfactory home. And they may well demonstrate the fact by dying.

A cold garden and a cold soil can be helped, as can all gardens, by careful planning and by using the right plants. This does not mean that all one's cherished hopes of growing this or that exotic must be thrown away. Parts of the garden can be protected to conserve the warmth of the sun and to deflect the wind, soil can be made less sticky and water retentive or, for some special plants, a raised bed can be made. Much can be done. And great pleasure is obtained in succeeding when the books, invariably pessimistic to preserve the authors' reputations, assure you that all is impossible!

Soil

The soil is the basic material on which every garden has to work and and the material which makes plant growth possible. It is a highly complicated mixture of inorganic debris broken down over thousands of years from parent rock plus the decomposed organic remains of plant and animal bodies. It has been moved and mixed by the action of ice-sheets and by water. It also contains a huge population of living organisms from bacteria to earthworms all reacting upon it. Depending upon the type of parent rock, the soil will differ in its chemical makeup. Those built upon old igneous rocks such as granite are likely to be acid (we can grow rhododendrons and camellias but our cabbages will be poor) whilst those on the soft sedimentary limestones and chalk will have the opposite reaction as they will be growing on an alkaline soil.

It is too simplistic to assert, as is so often done, that sandy soils are necessarily poor. Similarly, clay soils, whilst well known to be extremely difficult to work and slow to warm up, are not all bad. They can produce splendid crops with almost no supplementary feeding.

Air and Light

Of two other essentials for plant growth it would seem that there is no lack. Yet nowadays under glass it is common for the greenhouse atmosphere to be enriched by added carbon dioxide in order to increase the rate of photosynthesis (and hence growth) and to extend daylength artificially to the same end. In the open garden such possibilities do not occur but it does emphasise that, as with other factors, plants are adapted to succeed in every sort of position. There are those which are best in full sun, in dappled or full shade. It is much better to suit such plants to the position rather than to fight with what doesn't want to 'do'.

Water

Water is necessary to all plants – even cacti which have gone as far as any plant can in adaptation to manage with very little. Its use is two-fold; as a part of the photosynthesis process which builds up sugars and starches in the leaves as one source of the food needed for plant energy, and secondly, but vitally, as the medium in which chemical nutrients are taken up from the soil through the roots into the conducting tissues of every part of the plant. The problems posed by the necessary 'plumbing' of a big tree are worth a lot of thought, for it is the sufficiency of water which keeps all young plants or young parts of older plants upright. Cut off their water supply and they wilt and die.

Fortunately rainfall in Great Britain is usually adequate, at least in theory, for most of the plants we want to grow, though it varies from less than 60cm (24in) per annum to four times that amount in different parts of the country. Rainfall, however, is not the full story. How much of it is actually available to our plants may be quite another thing. So much will depend upon the water-holding capacity of the soil so that it is still there when plants need it during the important growth periods of spring and summer. Heavy clay soils hold too much water, but this is usually in the winter. Paradoxically, in summer it is often easier for relatively light soils to 'pull' water up from underground sources. The answer for the gardener is to try to develop his soil to drain excess water away while building up its organic complement with well-rotted manure or compost. This acts like a sponge and holds some moisture to be available to plants' roots at all times. Chalky and thin limestone soils have a continual problem here because organic compost and manure decomposes so quickly; but it is vital to persevere with improving them.

Exposed Sites

It can be seen then that working *within* the climate and the soil that the garden is blessed with, does not encourage mere fatalism. Amelioration is always possible in one form or another.

Another consideration in answer to a self-posed question of 'What have I got?' is that of exposure to the wind. The problem varies from seaside gardens where the first onslaught of spray-carrying gales has to be met, to small town gardens, apparently protected by high walls yet often vulnerable to wicked down-draughts and eddies roaring round the buildings.

The seaside or high hillside garden has very special problems. In the former case strong salt-laden winds are able to kill young leaves and soft growth of even native plants: I have seen the south side of hedges burned for miles inland by a late summer gale roaring up the valley from that direction. Clearly few plants can succeed in the front line, but there are a few. Again one must see what is successful already in the area and build upon that. Fortunately, the influence of the sea moderates low winter temperatures so that some suitable plants, too frost-tender for inland gardens, are available which might generally not be thought of. Even then, in the early years, a few carefully placed wattle hurdles may be necessary to give some protection.

Exposed hillside gardens have similar problems, but often without the comforting mildness of the seaside. The shape of any mature trees will show very graphically the direction and fierceness of the prevailing winds. But, and this factor must have consideration in all gardens, such sites have been chosen to put a house on because of the views of the seaside or its commanding position on the hill. The view is vital, it must never be planted out. In such situations protected corners can be contrived

to keep open the view whilst still providing a sheltered site for plants which would otherwise perish.

Humphry Repton

In the 1790's and the early years of the 19th century, the landscape gardener who took on the mantle of Capability Brown was Humphry Repton (he was, incidentally, the first to use that title of himself). As a skilled water-colourist, one of his great virtues for an unimaginative patron was that he invariably painted a picture of the garden to be improved and then a clever painted cut-out which lifted off to show what the finished scheme would look like. His clients found the method irresistible and many of his Red Books (Repton bound the paintings and the accompanying report in red Moroccan leather covers) still exist. What was particularly important with this method is that it emphasised what aspects of the scene would be best hidden and what would be better exposed to view. It's a fascinating game we can all try, even if we can't draw, cameras have now been invented and can take the place of the former.

Repton's Red-Book drawings were concerned, almost inevitably, with the broad landscape stretching out from the windows of a grand country house. They showed how a group of trees, for example, would be much more effective if increased to the size of a small wood; how a single fine oak would dominate a vista if the scrub round its base were removed; how the banks of a river or a lake might appear to best advantage; how to cut through a high hedgerow so that a distant church spire was brought into the garden scene.

But a famous pair of his drawings concerned his own little house at Gidea Park, Hare Street, now in Essex. Here he showed that by disguising the less pleasant features and bringing into view the best, even a small garden scene could be given new life.

Present-day Examples

In our small 20th-century gardens the emphasis seems always to have been upon disguising the compost heap, planting Russian vine over the garden shed or hiding the vegetables. This is only a part of what is necessary; if there is any scope at all one should always look beyond the boundaries; there might be something worth looking at some way off. A prime example of stealing a view existed in a friend's garden, coincidentally only a couple of hundred yards from where Repton's house used to stand. The back gardens of a 1920's housing estate bounded a small lawn-tennis club; all but one gardener rigorously kept up their end fences. My friend took his down and framed the gentle view with interesting plants. This use seemed to quadruple his garden.

On a somewhat grander scale a long narrow garden needed a feature as an eye-catcher to close the view. When some miserable fruit trees were removed it was possible to align the garden's vista on a magnificent Victorian campanile – in fact a pumping-house chimney – half a mile away.

These are exceptional cases – we are not all blessed with tennis-courts or architectural features (let alone fairies) at the bottom of the garden. But they reinforce the desirability of discovering 'What have I got?', and then making the most of it. The effort is worthwhile and endlessly fascinating.

The Shape of the Plot

It becomes necessary at some point between the 'What have I got?' and 'What do I want?' questions to get to work with tape measure, ruler, pencil and rubber and some squared paper.

Where to Start

Firstly measure up the plot with some care. Note the positions of existing garden features; paths, borders, buildings and especially existing shrubs and trees. Mark the orientation and record the amount and time of shade cast by the house, by plants and by those outside the boundaries. Show trees, not by just dots where the trunks are, but circles describing their spread.

Draw this out to scale. Initially a relatively small plan is suitable, but several copies are needed. If it is too time consuming to draw them individually do the first with all the information and take it to one of those copying machines and do a dozen. So armed one can play with a number of plans without rubbing each one out and losing its ideas, or making the single plan confusing.

Inevitably everyone has certain preconceptions of what is required of their garden and these will be in mind at the next stage. This is to view the site from all angles at which it will be seen including from the kitchen window or door, French windows and upstairs (note too what is particularly in view from next-door's upstairs if there is one: a certain privacy is a prime requirement for many of us). Then do the exercise from the other way round by looking back to the house. It may be agreeable enough but is likely to be less effective as a back-drop for the garden. Stack pipes and drain pipes, large areas of bare wall, all are a suitable case for horticultural treatment. More productively niches by the chimney breast may offer covetable spots for some splendid exotic or a table grape vine perhaps.

Building up the Picture

In this way it becomes possible to site some of the desiderata on the 'What do I want?' list. Much play is made in subsequent sections of this book on the out-of-doors-room concept of parts of a modern garden and this terrace or patio is a basic point at which to start. At this stage it is enough to sit about in a garden chair, regardless of the weather, to see what is in view or out of it at about 1 to 1.25 m (3 to 4ft) above the ground. It is apt to be dramatically different from what is seen in the standing position.

This is the time to try the Reptonian game mentioned in the first chapter of making a sketch or taking a photograph. Do this both from and to the positions of importance and then build up an accompanying sketch of what one bravely hopes will be the 'after' effect. One does not have to be able to draw well to outline the shape of a tree or two or outline the upper limit of an area of planting-to-be.

The Basic Rectangle

The ultimate restraint, of course, is the shape of the plot. And this, as has already been admitted in the vast number of cases today, is a simple rectangle behind the house some three or four times as long as it is broad. It is usually entirely separated from the front garden by the house itself so that the whole area can seldom be considered as a single unit.

The wider the plot the more the possibilities of interesting variations in design occur because there is a chance that several vistas or lines of sight can be contrived from the windows of the house. The basic rectangle seldom offers such potential, though sometimes it is possible to 'borrow' an eye catching tree or worthwhile building outside one's own domain, the view of which must be kept open.

A typical, logical layout is, to use a term current in modern motor-car construction, a 'three-box' one: terrace; lawn and flower borders; vegetables and fruit. Where the orientation from the house is south west round to due west, this is likely to be satisfactory. The inevitable formality of the hard materials – brick, stone or stucco that comprise the house moves towards the only partially less formal terrace with its stone floor and man-made retaining walls and furniture. This, however, should be softened by luxuriant plant growth spilling over the edges, climbing the walls and possibly roofing a part of the area as a pergola. Successful terrace planting is the visual door to a successful garden, for the terrace is seen and used the most of any part of the garden. Its design is, therefore, vital.

Size should be adequate for the sort of outside living that is intended. Although it should not overbalance the garden design as a whole it may well be dominant in a very limited area. Its extent, the position of integral beds or boundary planting, needs to be simple and logical: lines which already exist; the house gable, a bay window, even an immovable coal bunker are reasonable starting points for the layout and take their place to give the impression of inevitability, though if it is successful conscious thought will no longer be given to it. This slots into the next part of the garden and its view and access.

The second 'box' of lawn and flower borders is obviously less formal in texture and material than the terrace by which it is approached. Its furnishings, although utterly unnatural as far as arrangement is concerned, are mainly living organisms and as such have their own potential and habit to develop. The gardener's role is to choose plants which like his soil and climate (there is no point in putting rhododendrons at the top of the 'What do I want?' list if the garden is on chalk for instance). In doing this a selection is being made; a selection from the truly magnificent range of plants actually available.

For the successful garden design whether it is a 'basic rectangle', extending, as the house agents say '. . . in all to nearly one tenth of an acre . . .' or one of considerable size, this plethora of choice is a potential danger. Gertrude Jekyll put the point with characteristic force well over half a century ago; 'I am strongly of the opinion' she wrote, 'that the possession of a quantity of plants, however good the plants may be in themselves, does not make a garden. It only makes a collection.' And elsewhere Miss Jekyll states 'There is a duty we owe to our gardens' (which is to develop a) 'state of mind and artistic conscience that will not tolerate bad or careless combination or any misuse of plants.'

The problem is a complicated one and such high flown sentiments are not easy to live up to. Gardens with which this book is mainly concerned

are not likely to be big enough to have areas of separate seasonal interest, or an enclosed rose garden which can look like a heap of bare sticks for a third of the year without anyone complaining. Even more important then are the associations of plants in those areas which are to be cultivated. Oddly enough while most people take great care in the arrangements of plants when cut for the house, the same thought is not so frequent in the garden.

Plant Association
This is not just putting together a group of plants which flower at the same time; this might be just a bit of traditional red, white and blue summer bedding. Though, of course, the time factor is an important one. It is impossible, and certainly undesirable, to have a blaze of colour throughout the year; so emphasis is best made by contriving a series of small garden pictures.

So what are wanted are groups, sometimes only two or three plants which are complementary at any one time, each adding to the others' beauty and effectiveness. While shape, texture and leaf effect are all vital, much association is bound to be based upon flower colour. Much, too, is personal choice but general guidance can be given, though nothing to compare with actually observing the plants themselves and working with them. Certainly the assertion that 'flower colours don't clash' may be true enough in the wild; in the garden which is the accumulation of nature's and the hybridist's art it certainly has no validity at all.

A couple of good examples might be a pale yellow tree lupin with some clear blue flag irises; grey foliage of santolina or *Artemesia* 'Lambrook Silver' with a whole range of soft lilac and pale purple flowers. Bright scarlet and other 'hot' colours need especial care.

While such considerations are

always necessary much plant association suggests itself in what might be called an ecological fashion. Shade-loving ferns, primulas, hostas, *Smilacina racemosa* are inevitably 'right'. So too are plants of hot dry banks, cistus, lavender, rosemary, yuccas and so on. And in general 'species' plants (that is those wild in some parts of the world) are less difficult to deal with than the brighter garden hybrids. Often, too, they have a delicacy of form that the others lack.

These apparently specialist considerations are not immediately necessary to the design of the 'basic rectangle' but they are aspects which should be inherent in all that is planned.

Movement from lawn and flower garden is frequently to the economic 'bottom of the garden', the vegetables, fruit, garden shed, compost heap and bonfire corner. These last two factors are vital. There is always woody rubbish to dispose of and more importantly there is always organic material to compost. Not a leaf should be wasted that can be converted into humus to return to the soil. There are a number of bins currently on the market designed to compost tidily. Make sure the size is sufficient to take everything convertible (it may be better to construct two or three cubic metre (6 or 10 cubic feet) bays from old planks. As two mature one is ready to use).

A problem of this hypothetical basic rectangle is frequently its lack of depth. To divide the already small area into sections is potentially restrictive. Where possible therefore a main vista should stop as far as possible from the beginning of the sight line. This vista closing may well end at the tool shed: this is no worry if the shed is visually acceptable. If it is not then an attractive tree in front or a mural on the door may need to be considered. An amusing conceit is the construction of a *trompe de l'oeil* arch or gazebo at the end of the vista. A garden shed could well be its base. Well done it gives a splendid false perspective. The only thing to emphasise here is that no main sight line should end in anything unattractive. Nor need it.

Other Garden Shapes

Basic rectangles may be frequent but they do not encompass all small garden possibilities. Sometimes, especially with 19th-century houses, the garden is narrow and very long. Here a full length vista may seem entirely out of scale. A main view-line may end at a median point with hidden egress from that apparent end to further limits of the garden. Such gardens can be happily contrived as a series of small interconnecting rooms, each with its own emphasis or cultivational specialisation. Often such gardens, simply because of their age, have fine trees around which to base contemporary planning.

Here at least the constraints of the

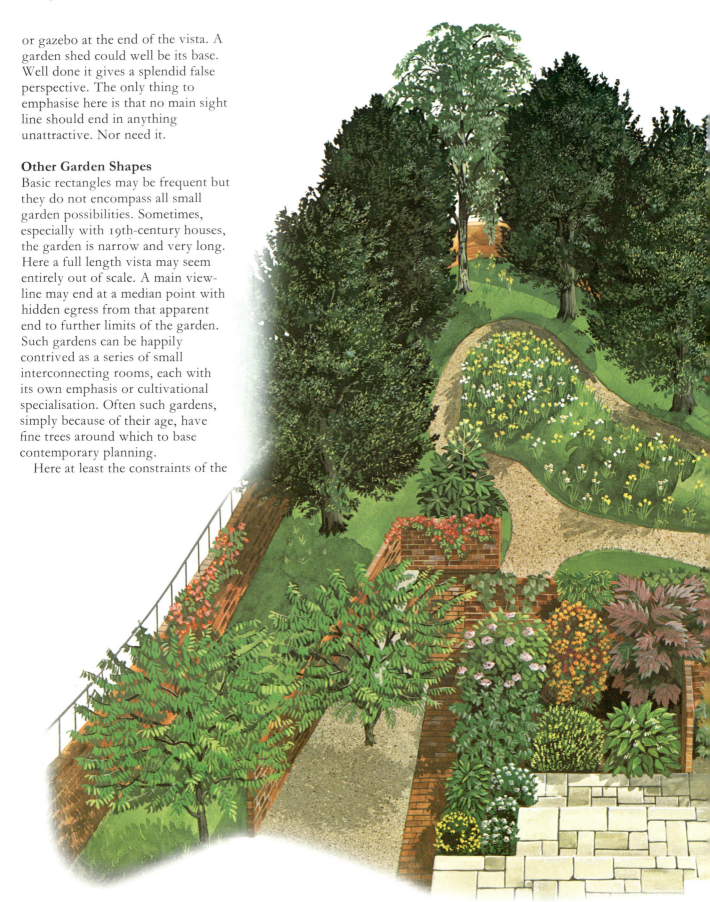

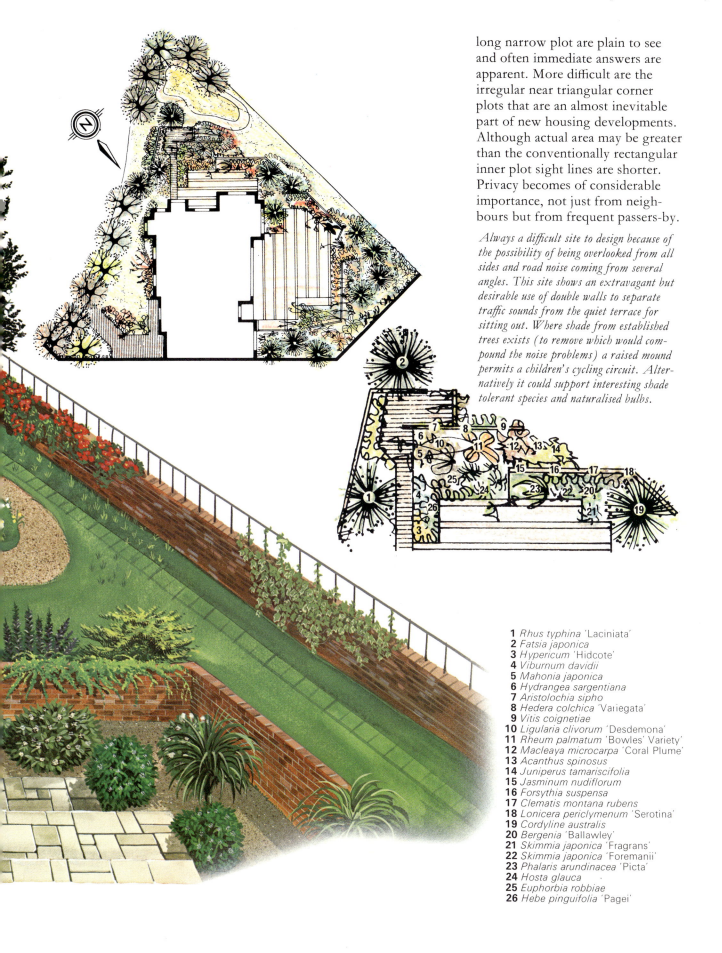

long narrow plot are plain to see and often immediate answers are apparent. More difficult are the irregular near triangular corner plots that are an almost inevitable part of new housing developments. Although actual area may be greater than the conventionally rectangular inner plot sight lines are shorter. Privacy becomes of considerable importance, not just from neighbours but from frequent passers-by.

Always a difficult site to design because of the possibility of being overlooked from all sides and road noise coming from several angles. This site shows an extravagant but desirable use of double walls to separate traffic sounds from the quiet terrace for sitting out. Where shade from established trees exists (to remove which would compound the noise problems) a raised mound permits a children's cycling circuit. Alternatively it could support interesting shade tolerant species and naturalised bulbs.

 1 *Rhus typhina* 'Laciniata'
 2 *Fatsia japonica*
 3 *Hypericum* 'Hidcote'
 4 *Viburnum davidii*
 5 *Mahonia japonica*
 6 *Hydrangea sargentiana*
 7 *Aristolochia sipho*
 8 *Hedera colchica* 'Variegata'
 9 *Vitis coignetiae*
10 *Ligularia clivorum* 'Desdemona'
11 *Rheum palmatum* 'Bowles' Variety'
12 *Macleaya microcarpa* 'Coral Plume'
13 *Acanthus spinosus*
14 *Juniperus tamariscifolia*
15 *Jasminum nudiflorum*
16 *Forsythia suspensa*
17 *Clematis montana rubens*
18 *Lonicera periclymenum* 'Serotina'
19 *Cordyline australis*
20 *Bergenia* 'Ballawley'
21 *Skimmia japonica* 'Fragrans'
22 *Skimmia japonica* 'Foremanii'
23 *Phalaris arundinacea* 'Picta'
24 *Hosta glauca*
25 *Euphorbia robbiae*
26 *Hebe pinguifolia* 'Pagei'

Range of Conditions and Sites

WHILE OTHER SECTIONS OF THIS book deal in rather greater detail with shady gardens and other sites posing particular problems it is worth considering the possible diversity of the garden scene. So often one is expected to be gardening on the classic 'deep, rich loam, well drained yet retentive of moisture' which every well-brought-up young plant appears to demand. This is sadly not true; as most of us do not. Soil and climate combine into a bewilderingly numerous range of types. It may be distressing that many gardens cannot be described as 'favoured', but the diversity precludes horticultural boredom – at least it would if more people were aware of the possibilities.

Soil

The basic material on which the success of a garden depends is, of course, its soil. In particular it is the topsoil which matters. Soil is a combination of inorganic rock detritus, gradually broken down by aeons of weathering, and organic material. This organic 'humus' is the product of decayed vegetable and animal matter worked upon by earthworms, bacteria and the other myriad underground creatures. Weathering and decomposition release the basic elements needed for plant growth. Manures and fertilisers supplement these foods and they are both more available and more concentrated in the topsoil.

Clay

However chemically rich a soil, plants will not be happy if its physical structure is not right. In addition to foods, plant roots need water and air. An excess of water means lack of air and a heavy impervious soil in which plant roots rot off and die. Clay soils have this dangerous potential. The particles of which clay soils are made are extremely small and hence hold much moisture in the interparticle spaces: double digging and the addition of plenty of humus will help drainage. But in very badly drained soils, where water lays for long periods after heavy rain, artificial drains below the soil surface may be the only solution. It is a common one in agriculture; however, back gardens do not get a government subsidy. It should be remembered that soil structure is very easily ruined by heavy machinery when houses are being built and even by excessive trampling. Clay soils have to be worked with when conditions permit; they cannot be fought.

Sandy Soil

Light, sandy soils are the opposite side of the coin. They are dry, as their large particles permit rapid drainage of water, and often poor because plant foods are washed out too. But they are easy to work, warming up quickly in spring. Plenty of additional organic matter here also helps to hold water like a sponge.

Loam

In between these extremes are the loams, which combine large and small particles and hence have the virtues of both. They have the potential for growing an extremely wide range of plants.

Acid or Alkaline

Another important factor about soil type is its being either acid or alkaline. This depends mainly upon the underlying rock of which the subsoil and ultimately the topsoil is a part. Granite produces an acid soil, chalk an alkaline or limy soil. It is measured, for convenience, on a scale of values called pH. In this, garden soils are likely to vary between pH 4, very acid, and pH 8.5 very limy. pH 7 is the neutral point.

pH is significant in that plant species are adapted to a certain soil type in their original wild habitat and succeed best when cultivated in a similar soil. Sometimes they are utterly unable to exist in any other way. Rhododendrons, camellias, heathers and other shrubs need an acid soil. Lime is anathema to them. Very few plants, however, insist on a high pH (though cabbages prefer it) and a soil just below pH 7 will permit the greatest range of plant species to be grown. Acid soils can be changed by adding calcium carbonate in some form, but a limy soil stays that way. The only practical method of growing calcifuge plants in a limy garden is to make raised beds filled with imported soil.

Climate

A garden soil is continually being affected by the weather: water is added or evaporated; frost helps to ameliorate heavy clay if it has been dug over in autumn and left rough for the winter; heat and drought cause it to crack in the summer. A successful gardener is one who is able to work happily within the climatic pattern of his garden.

England is in an extraordinary geographical position lying mainly between the fifty-degree and sixty-degree parallels. It enjoys a climate which is remarkable when it is realised that Edinburgh is about on a line with Moscow, and London is to the north of all Newfoundland. Yet the Scilly Isles can rival Madeira in plant materials. We are helped, as every schoolboy knows, by the Transatlantic Gulf Stream drift bringing relatively warm water from the Caribbean to our western shores. This is why gardens to the west of the country, even in the far north, offer marvellous opportunities to the plantsman.

The South and East have alternative advantages. The nearness to the sea prevents extremes of temperature, but stronger sun and drier climate encourage plants from Mediterranean countries. All the aromatic herbs enjoy these conditions and plants grown for autumn colour are particularly fine.

It is from these differences that our marvellous diversity of plants follows. Fortunately in all but the wettest and coldest areas, the whole range of well-loved garden plants, from roses and delphiniums to pinks and peonies do marvellously well. What is necessary is to appreciate any particular problems and, especially, potentials and to capitalise upon them.

This map shows England to have a maritime-type climate which is governed by the warm water brought by the Transatlantic Gulf Stream. It ensures warmer winters and cooler summers than those which exist in the transitional and continental regions, whose winters are sub-zero and summers are hotter than on the coast. Maritime areas also have rain all the year round rather than the seasonal, fairly low rainfall, by contrast, of the continental interiors.

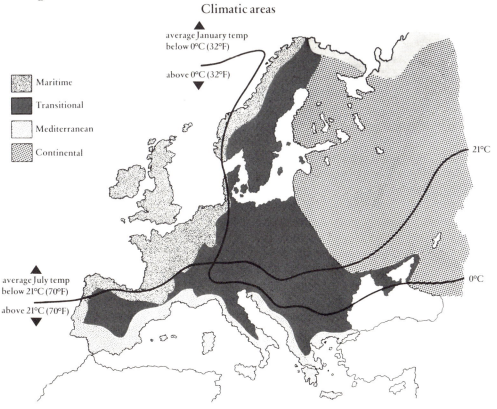

Climatic areas

▲ average January temp below 0°C (32°F)

▼ above 0°C (32°F)

Maritime

Transitional

Mediterranean

Continental

21°C

0°C

▲ average July temp below 21°C (70°F)

▼ above 21°C (70°F)

The Shared Garden

It is not unusual nowadays for gardens to be shared by different members of a family living in separate parts of the same house or even different families sharing a building and hence the garden as well. This is the principle upon which many fine old town square gardens are based and also much more recent domestic planning where each house has a small private courtyard or patio which gives on to a communal area beyond.

There is much sense in this because of the difference in scale of design and planting that is both necessary and desirable – the close, easily-maintained area of the adjacent out-door room leading from the house and the treed open space beyond, looked after professionally or by mutual efforts of the residents who share it. Such an arrangement is one that has saved many houses in the suburbs and the country, now too large for single ownership, from demolition with the consequent loss of their gardens. These in turn have been divided for all residents to share. It is important that, while not every window can look down upon its own garden, each should have an area which is quite private – even if this is quite small.

Unfortunately division of the garden is apt to be given much less thought than division of the house, but it is no less important to the creation of successfully shared buildings.

The plan here represents a much simpler situation, but one which is not uncommon.

1 *Betula pendula*
2 *Camellia* 'J. C. Williams'
3 *Erica lusitanica*
4 *Berberis calliantha*
5 *Euonymus radicans* 'Silver Queen'
6 *Daboecia cantabrica*
7 *Genista cinerea*
8 *Hebe pinguifolia* 'Pagei'
9 *Coronilla glauca*
10 *Lavendula*
11 *Santolina pectinata*
12 *Ruta* 'Jackman's Blue'
13 *Laurus nobilis*
14 *Thymus*
15 *Chamaerops humilis*
16 Exotic bulbs
17 *Leycesteria formosa*
18 *Cistus x cyprius* underplanted with *Convallaria majalis*
19 *Cistus x skanbergii*
20 *Phormium tenax*
21 *Euphorbia rigida*
22 *Fatsia japonica*
23 *Acanthus spinosus*
24 *Yucca gloriosa*
25 *Arundinaria nitida*
26 *Rhododendron mucronulatum*
27 *Erica carnea* 'Vivellii'

A biggish Victorian semi-detached house has a 'granny flat' using some of the ground floor. From the sitting room of this flat doors open onto its own small sitting-out area which catches some early sun – perhaps up to lunch time. From here a path, angled to give a feeling of space, moves through dense planting and under a vine-draped pergola before coming into sight of the main garden which has its own entrance to the second, main, house unit. Cohesion of the two gardens in one has been encouraged by using the same brick throughout – yellow London stock – of which the house was built a hundred years ago and which it will soon match.

As much round-the-year interest of plants in flower, foliage and texture as possible has been provided taking care to use each aspect to its optimum potential.

The Town Garden

BECAUSE OF PRESSURE OF SPACE THE smallest area of garden in a town is worth making the most of. It is not many years ago since winter smogs so blackened leaves and depressed plants and people alike that small town gardens were hardly thought worthwhile. Reduction of atmospheric pollution has changed all that so much so that many town gardens enjoy conditions which a country garden might well envy. Any large conurbation raises ambient temperatures and reduces humidity – and while the latter is a horticultural misfortune, on a small scale it is very easily remedied. But the warmer temperatures, especially in winter, are invaluable.

An Outdoor Room

Sun is bound to be at a premium because of the likelihood of surrounding high walls and other buildings, and this is bound to dictate much of the design of the garden. Desirable though it is, even if a town garden enjoys virtually no sun at all it is enormously worthwhile to make an attractive garden in the space that is available. Think of it as a cool evening sitting-room for use after work. To be able to be outside at the end of a stifling summer's day is the restorative experience that every city dweller needs. It is sad so few have the opportunity.

It is likely, therefore, that the small size of town gardens makes it necessary that every inch is used to advantage. It is usually best considered as a terrace or 'patio' from which there is no way out, in other words an enclosed courtyard, where the 'views' have to be contrived by the use of interesting plants on the walls or carefully arranged objects. An illusion of space can be contrived by a wall-painting or white-painted trellis built in false perspective. Wherever possible a view from a window or a door should appear to go somewhere or end in a definite way. A wall-mask dripping water into a shell is an unoriginal, but always delightful eye catcher.

Town dwellers invariably pine for grass, but it is a great mistake to try to maintain a necessarily minute lawn in a town garden. Good lawn grasses are just not adapted to shade and invariably die out: annual meadow grass comes in which is incapable of remaining green throughout the year and the result is a mess. There is, then, no alternative to hard surfaces of one sort or another – paving and brick where people are to walk or sit, cobbles or loose gravel where contrast is required to the planted areas around.

Planting

Good permanent planting is vital to give texture and body throughout the year. Leaf shape and general outline are often more important than beauty of flower. But the two are not mutually exclusive. Camellias are marvellous town plants in all but the coldest spots. Their lustrous evergreen leaves, tidy habit, heavy autumn buds full of pregnant potential opening to luxurious flowers, make them invaluable. They make good wall plants (back branches tied to the support) and exist in a range of colours from white to dark blood red.

Their only reservation is an insistence on acid soil and if this is not natural (although many old town soils become so) a raised bed of imported lime-free soil plus peat is a good investment. The modern *Camellia x williamsii* hybrids are particularly lovely, the singles having a delicate dog-rose grace. Camellias will take full shade and still flower: only really hot, dry spots should be avoided.

Climbers

There are very few self-clinging climbers. Virginia creeper in one of its forms attains the greatest height (when it really gets rather unmanageable) but has the disadvantage of being deciduous. This is true, also, of the otherwise lovely climbing *Hydrangea petiolaris*. The most valuable plant for town garden walls (and not only these) is ivy in all its many forms; green, gold, variegated, big leaved or small leaved. It is worth mentioning, too, that contrary to popular belief,

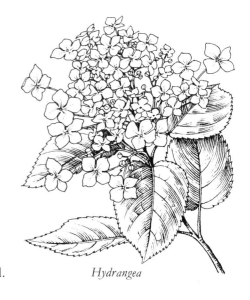

Hydrangea

ivy does not harm sound walls at all – though it will get into cracks and under slates as will any climber given the chance.

All other climbers will need support round which they can twine (summer jasmine and wisteria) or can hold onto (vines and clematis) and this should be done as permanently as possible. A difficulty occurs here with white or colour-washed walls, although in dark courtyards the whiteness does help to lighten the effect, for when repainting is necessary the climbers are in the way. One answer is not to worry but just to let the plants furnish the 'room', another is to have wires strung from upright battens which are hinged at the base; the whole section can then be swung out and down, the plant stems being flexible enough to accept this.

Covering the Ground

At the foot of the climbers a miscellany of plants, shrubby and herbaceous will follow. Again the ideal is complete cover – soil is a medium for growing plants in, not an aesthetic experience in its own right. Summer colour is best added by containers of annuals, including scented things such as tobacco plants, petunias and stocks with the more unusual pelargoniums (which are marvellous town-garden plants: in London they often survive the winter) and fuschias. Sadly very few roses are good town garden plants when mixed with other things. They become leggy and look dreadful in winter. Climbing roses too are apt to get quite out of reach and are a considerable effort to train and prune. An exception is the lovely, thornless *Rosa banksiae*. It is a plant for a south-facing, two- or three-storey house and gives cascades of small double yellow flowers in May and June.

Growing Food

There is no reason why town

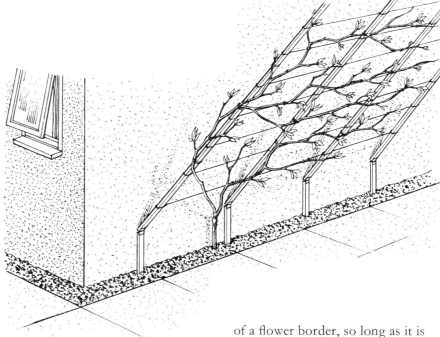

Climbers on a colour-washed or rendered wall which is going to need periodic attention can be difficult. Do not let this be a reason for not clothing walls, hinged panels give the answer.

gardeners should be denied the pleasures of their own edible produce. The warmth of an enclosed courtyard is ideal for a trained fig and its leaves make a lovely pattern against a plain wall. Several varieties of grapes succeed admirably. More mundane, but no less acceptable on the table, are runner beans. These started life here as ornamental plants and they really do look well with their large leaves and scarlet flowers. Town courtyards are also good for containers of sweet peppers and, of course, tomatoes. A currently effective method is the plastic bag of nutrient-impregnated peat which you slit and plant up. Unfortunately, plastic bags gaily advertising their makers hardly add to the scene, but with care their utilitarian brashness can be disguised.

Fresh herbs are invaluable. The shrubby types, rosemary, thyme, savory are happy in the miscellany of a flower border, so long as it is sunny. Mint is best in a shady corner, well separated from other things because it can take over an area in no time. Parsley can be scattered anywhere it will grow, as the leaves are always good to look at as to eat.

Easy to Care For

The great virtue of a small town garden is that it can be looked after easily without much exertion. With effort, on the other hand, every individual plant can be cared for and really remarkable results obtained. One factor does need to be kept in mind. Luxuriant plant growth from a small area of soil does naturally tend to deplete it: generous foliar feeding with a proprietary liquid plant food is very necessary and a small compost heap where every bit of garden and kitchen refuse is kept should be seriously considered. There are enclosed containers now available which could sit in the dustbin corner and provide a continual amount of organic material.

If there is only a small garden and the owner is keen on plants, there is a very natural tendency to use too many single species to get a really good general effect. A better

1 *Acer hersii*
2 Woodland plants: *Smilacina racemosa*
 Polygonatum multiflorum
 Convallaria majalis
 Liriope muscari
3 *Prunus x hilleri* 'Spire'
4 *Clematis macropetala* over
 Pyracantha lalandei
5 *Eccremocarpus scaber* over
 Cotoneaster horizontalis
6 *Hydrangea petiolaris*
7 *Lonicera japonica halliana*
8 *Iris pallida aurea*
9 *Hosta fortunei glauca*
10 *Laburnum alpinum*
11 *Liriope muscari*
12 *Bergenia* 'Ballawley'
13 *Lunaria annua*
14 *Potentilla* 'Elizabeth'
15 *Lamiastrum galeobdolon* 'Variegatum'
16 *Ajuga* 'Burgundy Glow'
17 *Phormium tenax* 'Purpurea'
18 *Juniperus* 'Skyrocket'
19 *Cornus alba* 'Aurea'
20 *Berberis thunbergii* 'Atropurpurea'
21 *Euonymus* 'Silver Queen'
22 *Euphorbia wulfenii*
23 *Prunus cistena*
24 *Philadelphus coronarius aureus*
25 *Rosa* 'Emily Grey'
26 *Rosa* 'Penelope'
27 *Rosa* 'Mermaid'
25, 26, 27 underplanted with spring
bulbs and polyanthus
28 *Laurus nobilis*

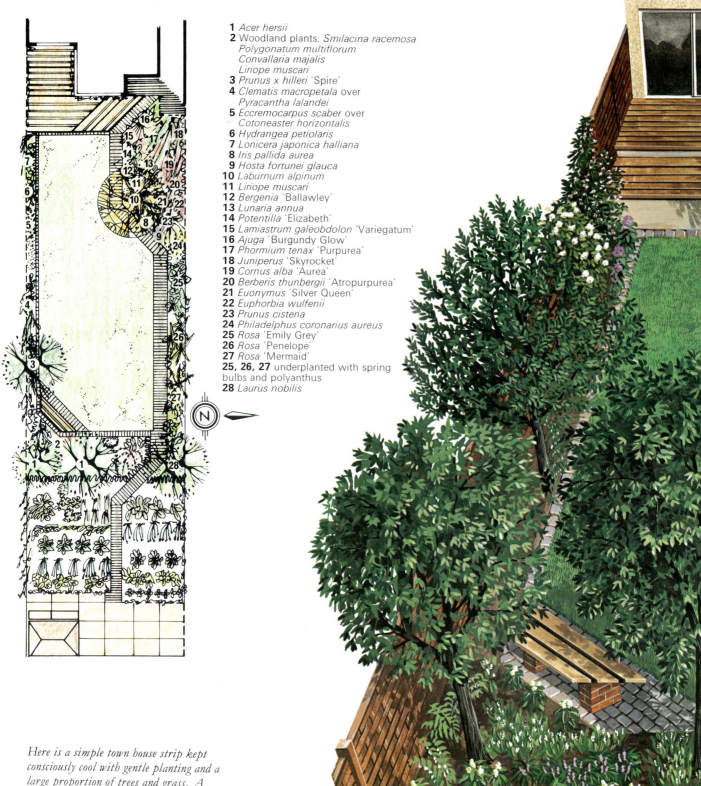

*Here is a simple town house strip kept
consciously cool with gentle planting and a
large proportion of trees and grass. A
country-garden feeling is aimed at with the
path leading perhaps into a field or coppice
rather than into the small kitchen garden.
Trees are encouraged to grow naturally, the
multi-stemmed laburnum providing light
shade and elegant shape both before and after
its three weeks of glory.*

analogy, however, is with the drawing room indoors: this may possess fine furniture strewn with dearly loved collections of glass and porcelain and so on. But unless some restraint is shown in the number of objects and unless the groups are complementary, the effect is of a magpie accumulation.

This is not to pursue the purist idea to absurdity, merely to emphasise the need for a general as well as a particular eye. In choosing plants for a restricted space their all-year-round value should be assessed. The now well-known winter flowering shrub *Mahonia japonica* is a case in point. This is a plant of superb shape and habit with great cartwheels of glossy leaves, which, in spite of being evergreen often colour beautifully in autumn. In October long trails of pale primrose-yellow flowers start to open, they are deliciously scented, and there will be some out until the following April. New shoot growth then begins which is soft and of a delicate powdery purple colour, gradually attaining the strength of the fully grown leaves. Altogether a remarkable plant which is not fussy as to soil and will accept both sun and shade.

Obviously few plants are such paragons and there is a danger that they become overused to the point at which familiarity breeds contempt, nonetheless they should be sought. And in the seeking some plants will appeal particularly and personally to oneself and earn their all-round keep because of it. It may be, for example, that deep-purple lilac is a top favourite plant without which a garden would hardly be wanted. If that is the case no more need be said. But if, on the other hand, it is not a major passion the question should be asked whether this big bush, albeit lovely for three weeks of the year, justifies its ugly leaves for six months and its bare branches of no particular merit for the other six.

The Country Garden

THERE IS AN ARCHETYPAL IMAGE OF the ideal country garden; from a sleepy lane, a gate in a low wall shows a broad flagged path leading to the venerable door of a black and white thatched cottage. The path is cascaded with flowers, pinks burgeon from cracks in the paving and roses are so prolific over the porch that everyone of normal size has to go round to the back door. The idyllic picture is not without validity but it should be realised that such effects are in almost every case the product of much care and hard work and that they are also the result, not of romantic recreation of a past period of rustic perfection but 20th-century gardening in one of its better forms.

The important point is that it is lovely to look at and that it works by giving the impression of being absolutely right in its context. This surely is one of the main criteria of garden success in any context. In the country, fitting a garden into its scene is particularly important. But we do not all live in black-and-white-timbered cottages. Outskirts of country towns and villages are now peppered with contemporary houses and bungalows in the conventional convenient style which hardly varies throughout the country.

A Natural Effect
What does help always to settle a house into its site is a successful garden. In towns and built-up areas there is little need to worry greatly unless there is a definite local style or material to build upon. In the country making an effort to fit in with the scene is so much more important; if there is a local stone available at a reasonable price it really should be used for garden walls or paving. Sometimes, as in the Cotswolds, there is good (and bad) artificial stone, coloured to fit in with old buildings. In many cases, unfortunately, houses and walls constructed of such material do look very brash – perhaps we should wait without impatience for time to mellow them but meanwhile luxuriant planting will help a lot. This is especially necessary at points where a new wall joins an old one.

While a traditional cottage garden can take a riot of summer colours because of its essential unsophistication, it is very difficult to obtain such an effect by design. Better to go about things rather more quietly, especially if a new house is not to overassert itself. While not advocating a pedantically purist approach it is safe to suggest that the more strident effects of the hybridists' art, 'Super Star' roses, *Prunus* 'Kanzan', *Salvia splendens* cultivars and so on, do look over-aggressive in the country. Gentler reds amongst modern hybrid tea roses such as 'Fragrant Cloud' and 'Rosemary Rose' fit in much better, as does *Prunus sargentii* which also has a bonus of magnificent autumn colour.

The effect to aim at surely, is of controlled luxuriance where a carefully chosen miscellany of plants builds up the garden picture. This is not an art easily acquired and it is wise to refer to the masters, or mistresses of it. Much will be found in the books of the late Margery Fish and in those of Christopher Lloyd.

A peacock butterfly on Sedum spectabile *'Autumn Joy' is one of the great pleasures of that season. This lovely creature, with red admirals and tortoiseshells, can be encouraged into the garden by flowers like this and buddleia whose nectar they find attractive. Their caterpillars feed on nettles where the eggs are laid so try to leave a clump in a disregarded corner to ensure the next generation of butterflies.*

There is always attraction and charm in so-called old-fashioned flowers. The term is pretty vague and is apt to include a lot of things which our ancestors never knew: its antithesis, however, is clear enough and two or three examples of such plants are mentioned above. What are meant, obviously, are plants of the countryside (ours and other people's); foxgloves, auriculas, dog daisies, hollyhocks, pinks, poly-anthus, Madonna lilies amongst herbaceous planting. Shrub roses, philadelphus, hydrangeas and fuchsias come to mind amongst shrubs. This is not to suggest leaving out hosts of garden-worthy plants from all over the world, possibly of quite recent introduction. In general, as one might expect, plants of wild origin – those referred to as species – are likely to fit in the best.

Birds in the Garden

One of the particular pleasures of country gardening to most people is the variety of wild life which becomes associated with the garden. Smiles become a little forced when mice eat every crocus corm and blackbirds start queuing up at the one tear in the raspberry netting, but these are universal rural hazards. Some form of *modus vivendi* is certainly necessary both in town and country, and that is to grow all soft fruit, except gooseberries, in a cage. Modern models, with metal uprights and nylon or polypropylene netting easily removed and stored after the fruit has been picked, are expensive but effective and long lasting. In some areas similar protection will have to be given to brassica crops from voracious pigeons, especially in winter if a single Brussels sprout is to be picked. Only tightly strung black cotton has any real effect, though it has to be renewed quite often. Scarecrows and various windmills are usually more fun for the children than a deterrent to the birds.

To look on the bright side, encouraging a range of beautiful and beneficial birds is both sensible and a pleasure. To watch blue tits scouring twigs and branches of trees is to realise what huge quantities of insects they consume. In addition, then, to the obvious bird table and water bath placed a couple of yards from a window where it is easily seen, a range of plants may be chosen to increase bird life. Tight laid or clipped hedges offer nesting sites, as do wall climbers and nesting boxes can be added. Autumn berrying shrubs such as cotoneasters, pyracanthas and berberis will attract finches. (If you don't want the berries eaten it is wise to plant yellow-fruited forms: birds leave these alone for months, presumably thinking them unripe.) Incidentally, greenfinches will gobble up every berry of *Daphne mezereum* as soon as it is ripe in August.

While the tamer birds will come to a fully exposed bird table, it will be used regularly by shy species if there is a nearby tree or large shrub for them to perch in and be sure the coast is clear and cat free before flying down. A range of food will encourage a diversity of feeders. Unfortunately starlings and sparrows are now learning a few acrobatics, once the preserve of the tits, that will provide them with equally high-grade protein as they steal nuts and fat from hanging containers. Ring the changes here and the tits will usually find the new food source that little bit quicker. The simplest form of bird table is just a board 45 by 30cm (18 by 12in) with a small branch attached on a leg

Polyanthus like multi-coloured primroses with large heads of flowers are a certain spring favourite. While size and colour range of the newer hybrids are stunning, making them fine pot plants for cool homes, the older smaller forms are better for outdoors where they can be massed in beds or grouped with spring bulbs in light shade.

1.4 to 1.5 m (4ft 6in to 5ft). This is sufficient to hold the food and a bowl of ice-free water. Birds are not better served by a pretty thatched house on a stick; on the contrary they are less able to watch out for predators.

Encouraging Butterflies

While it is delightful, especially in really cold weather, to know that one is really helping the survival of small birds, it is reasonable to expect something of a return on the family nut-fund. Feeding should cease when spring has really come in order that the birds should contribute to the general balance of nature in the garden by eating aphids and other insects. Fortunately not all insects are harmful and, of these, butterflies are not generally eaten by birds. So there is no clash of interests if there is an attempt to encourage butterflies into the garden. One of the great pleasures of late summer and early autumn – now sadly reduced from a couple of decades ago – is the number of

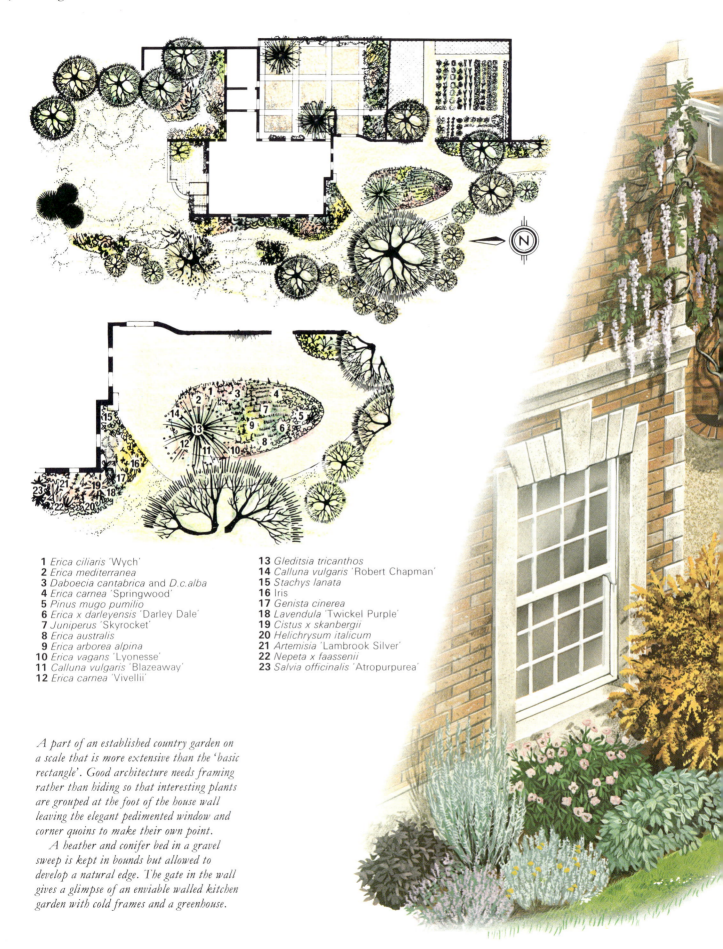

1 *Erica ciliaris* 'Wych'
2 *Erica mediterranea*
3 *Daboecia cantabrica* and *D.c.alba*
4 *Erica carnea* 'Springwood'
5 *Pinus mugo pumilio*
6 *Erica x darleyensis* 'Darley Dale'
7 *Juniperus* 'Skyrocket'
8 *Erica australis*
9 *Erica arborea alpina*
10 *Erica vagans* 'Lyonesse'
11 *Calluna vulgaris* 'Blazeaway'
12 *Erica carnea* 'Vivellii'

13 *Gleditsia tricanthos*
14 *Calluna vulgaris* 'Robert Chapman'
15 *Stachys lanata*
16 Iris
17 *Genista cinerea*
18 *Lavendula* 'Twickel Purple'
19 *Cistus x skanbergii*
20 *Helichrysum italicum*
21 *Artemisia* 'Lambrook Silver'
22 *Nepeta x faassenii*
23 *Salvia officinalis* 'Atropurpurea'

A part of an established country garden on a scale that is more extensive than the 'basic rectangle'. Good architecture needs framing rather than hiding so that interesting plants are grouped at the foot of the house wall leaving the elegant pedimented window and corner quoins to make their own point.

A heather and conifer bed in a gravel sweep is kept in bounds but allowed to develop a natural edge. The gate in the wall gives a glimpse of an enviable walled kitchen garden with cold frames and a greenhouse.

tortoiseshell, red admiral and peacock butterflies feeding from the flowers. Certain species are known to be especially attractive to them – buddleia is not known as butterfly bush for nothing. So to group a buddleia (*B. fallowiana* 'Lochinch' or *B.f. alba* are smaller, choicer forms with good grey foliage) with *Sedum spectabile* and early Michaelmas daisies will ensure that some of the butterfly population visit the garden.

Reduction in their numbers is commonly, and in the main rightly, blamed upon the general use of insecticides. Another is the over-zealous gardener and also the over-tidiness of local councils who immorally spray herbicides on road banks and hedgerows. It is generally forgotten that these butterflies, elegantly sipping at nectar, are the product of their caterpillar larval stage, heartily champing at nettle leaves. A patch of nettles, then, in a corner of the orchard or against a hedge could be the source of much autumn pleasure. It is also the source of a spring vegetable: boiled nettle tops, very young, are not at all bad.

Sloping Garden

WHEN ONE CONSIDERS THE enormous, but entirely worthwhile effort which has to be put into giving a flat garden the invaluable interest of contours, anyone with a sloping site should bless his lucky stars – or the ice age. Because there is no doubt that the visual and actual movement offered by banks, steps and ramps adds immeasurably to a garden. Nevertheless as in everything all is not light and joy; maintenance can be difficult and access complicated. Yet if the situation is taken from the first as being essentially desirable, it almost certainly will become so.

The ideal site, of course, is one which falls from the house to the south or south-west. Such spots catch all the sun and, what is often most important, warm up early in spring. The fact that the house is to the north and somewhat higher conveniently provides protection from the coldest quarters as well. Keen gardeners moving house could do worse than to search for such a position. Any place with these advantages must capitalise upon them: sun-loving Mediterranean plants on the terrace, tender climbers (relative to the part of the country concerned) on the house. It would be immoral not to use such opportunities to extend the usual range of plants seen.

Associated with this type of site is the likelihood of a worthwhile view stretching out below and ahead. This in turn causes problems of exposure to every wind which blows from the open quarter. Keeping the view or protecting the place are not easily reconcilable. Fortunately the choice is not usually so absolutely black and white, but if it has to be taken the balance is best made in favour of the view, finding plants which accept the conditions. Happily this is not really difficult. Exposed sites are discussed further in a separate section.

Problems of Cultivation

As with any site an early decision has to be made concerning the amount of ground to be actually cultivated, whether this is for flower borders or vegetables. On sloping terrain the decision is especially vital for while it is not difficult to find good plants to cover banks permanently it is not reasonable to expect frequently to dig or hoe any slope of more than a one in ten incline. Even this is much steeper than desirable. The disadvantages are obvious. Apart from the physical difficulties of actually doing the work, soil is washed down the slope during periods of heavy rain and, much more insidiously, there is a continual leaching of plant foods from the upper part of the piece of ground to the lower. If the slope does not end here there is then a continual nagging pain: the knowledge that one is fertilising next door's garden. Few things could be more maddening – especially if their vegetables are recognisably better. Small things, such as running rows *along* the contours, rather than up and down the slope, and digging similarly help to prevent serious run off, but can only be taken as something of a cosmetic palliative.

Terracing

The answer is obvious: to terrace. Only the expense and effort has prevented the statement being made earlier. But the nettle has to be grasped, perhaps literally. The days are well past when a couple of local men would dig away for half a winter at little cost; today has brought in their stead a JCB excavator which can remove most of the garden in a day. Such aids, employed with care, make the problems of terracing much less daunting. A skilled operator can work one of these dinosaur-like creatures as delicately as one can wish, but it is vital that he knows exactly what is required. Vital, too, is care with established trees. Everyone knows that excess root damage will weaken and even kill a tree but less care is often given to ensuring that none of the trunk is buried when earth moving takes place. If the level of soil is to be raised and a mature tree kept, it will need its own surrounding retaining wall to maintain the same soil level.

Topsoil is invaluable – it has taken millennia to build up as the perfect medium for growing plants – it must not be lost. Even under a few inches of subsoil it loses its structure and full value. This, then, must be scraped off the area to be terraced and safely stacked. The operation which follows is one of cutting and filling – a lower 'wedge' lifted and reversed on to that above, giving an upper and lower horizontal area separated by a vertical 'wall'. The topsoil is then returned.

Retaining Walls

This gross simplification needs a certain amplification. Firstly, if natural structure and drainage of the soil is not to be impaired, imovement of any large machinery must be as restricted as is consistent with doing the job. Secondly, the new vertical face of soil does not, naturally, stay up by itself. A retaining wall has to be constructed and steps will be necessary to link the upper and lower levels.

As discussed in the section on paved areas, steps and construction of walls near to the house should, be in similar materials to it or in something complementary. And while this is still desirable with retaining walls, where the slope falls from the house any such wall will be hidden from it; this does provide a certain leeway. Walls built above ground only have to support themselves, but it must be realised that retaining walls have a very definite job to do – the supporting of a great volume and weight of soil. Foundations must be adequate, weep-holes provided to permit drainage and an inward-leaning batter to help balance the weight of the soil.

Where the height is not too great (1.25 m [4ft] is about right) retaining walls can be of the uncemented dry-wall type. To do this well is an art indeed but to do it acceptably (if one's standards are not impossibly high) is well within the capability of any week-end gardener, and it becomes a fascinating ploy. Obtaining natural stone from any distance is extremely expensive: terracing above a rocky subsoil however, frequently produces a considerable proportion of the wherewithal. This should be so used whenever possible.

Upward Sloping Site

Much more of a problem is when the site slopes upwards to the north from the back of the house. (As this implies a fall from the front, an area around the front door becomes a possible place for a sitting-out area if relative privacy can be contrived:

there is no law to say that one *must* sit out only behind the house.) In such a case light is at a premium. The terrace level should be taken out as far as practicable, but realising that in doing so the retaining wall when it is reached may have to be aggressively high. Better perhaps is having a 2 to 3m wide (6 to 10ft) 'terrace' and then constructing a series of shelves like a wide flight of stairs across the full front of the site. This would make a marvellous rock garden with cascading plants falling over each level and facing the windows.

Sloping sites either nearly nullify or exaggerate the size of plants chosen to give privacy or shelter. Planted at the bottom of a sloping garden, trees may have to get to near-maturity (and take a century to do it) before they rise above the line of sight from the top terrace, while conversely relatively small shrubs take on an altogether unwonted importance when planted at or above eye level. Privacy may have to be contrived in small areas and planting, hedging or walling kept very close indeed. Similarly positions of greenhouses and other garden buildings need especial care if they are not to impinge too much upon the scene.

Obviously not all parts of a sloping garden can be terrace: nor indeed is it desirable. Informal planting on sloping ground, so long as it is not precipitous, is always full of interest. Maintenance, however, can be difficult and where space permits trees and shrubs under-planted with bulbs are best in rough grass. Paths or rides can then be mown where necessary. Consideration will need to be given to using machines capable of taking the extra effort of uphill work.

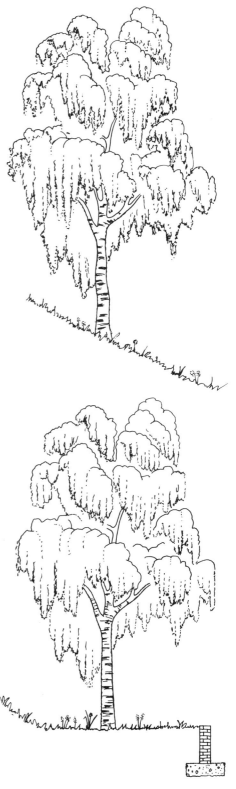

When terracing a sloping site remember to avoid changing the soil level around a tree. To overcome this problem a shelf should be constructed which will need to be supported by a retaining wall.

Planting a Slope

Where stone or brick terracing is inappropriate or merely impossibly expensive, the divide between two flat areas has to be a bank. This cannot be satisfactorily secure with a more than 45-degree slope; 30-degree is better but, of course, uses more space. Again there are problems of maintenance: grassed banks can look lovely but to be reasonable in an age when spare time seems always to be at a premium first class lawn quality is best replaced by use of the invaluable air-cushioned mower. Set it low and it can do a marvellous job and high banks can be dealt with by letting it down on a rope (vital, also, for safety, if toes are to be cared for).

Alternatively, many ground-cover plants provide trouble-free bank cover and often flower as well. *Hypericum calycinum* and *Cotoneaster microphylla* are good examples and there are several superb horizontal-growing junipers which seem made for this job.

Although changes in level are difficult to plan and inevitably more expensive to deal with, the potential is always vastly greater than on a flat site. Here the more convenient possibility of ground falling away from the house is shown. This is still the basic rectangle, but the raised terrace, flight of steps and the unusual angled paths set it apart from the simpler flat areas.

The terrace is laid with brick framing strips of paving which are repeated in the stepping-stone flagged path set diagonally across the lawn to the kitchen garden door. Such strong lines both accept and call for strong planting of interestingly shaped and textured plants.

1 *Salvia officinalis* 'Variegata'
2 Rosmarinus
3 *Salvia officinalis* 'Atropurpurea'
4 *Cistus x cyprius*
5 *Genista aetnensis*
6 *Camellia* 'J. C. Williams'
7 *Phalaris arundinacea* 'Picta'
8 *Milium effusum* 'Aureum'
9 Bergenia
10 *Elaeagnus pungens* 'Maculata'
11 Kniphofia
12 *Hedera colchica* 'Dentata Variegata'
13 *Fatsia japonica*
14 *Prunus x hillieri* 'Spire'
15 *Lilium martagon*
16 *Vinca minor*
17 *Arundinaria nitida*
18 Polygonatum
19 *Hosta glauca*
20 *Cortaderia argentea*
21 *Phormium tenax*
22 *Hosta* 'Thomas Hogg'
23 Lavendula
24 *Aralia elata*
25 *Elaeagnus pungens* 'Maculata'
26 *Hedera canariensis* 'Variegata'
27 *Camellia* 'Apple Blossom'
28 *Fatsia japonica*

Exposed Sites

IT HAS ALREADY BEEN SUGGESTED that in many cases a garden exposed to wind is so because the house of which it is a part has been expressly sited to make the most of a desirable view. Thoughts about a garden are apt to follow later; this is unfortunate but understandable. Yet as a distant prospect of the countryside or seascape is valuable beyond rubies to the environment of house and garden as a whole; it is positively agoraphobic to cut it off. So a balance has to be struck.

The problems are two-fold. These are the providing of sheltered areas for growing flowers and vegetables and for sitting in – there is nothing so cooling as a keen breeze over the hopefully browning back – and the ensuring that the view is kept open from the main windows of the house. The first decision, therefore, is to answer that old but vital question: What do I want? Should the sitting room open onto an enclosed patio as an extension of the house for sun-warmed living. Or should a decision permit the eye to travel to the horizon, accepting the corollary that sitting out will have definite limitations. It depends very much what sort of life one leads. Fortunately the two are not quite mutually exclusive and most people will opt for some combination of these facets.

Coping with Exposure

An exposed garden will certainly need to be compartmentalised to provide sheltered corners for plants which resent wind. Obviously notice carefully what does well in the area but it is also wise to think, when choosing plants for windy sites (or indeed any other), in what might be called an ecological way. All plants in the wild are adapted to their habitat. In this situation choose maritime plants or mountain plants for positions of full exposure. Those from bosky woodlands or damp valleys will be avoided or especially catered for in contrived protection. The general habits of plants tell us a lot about their requirements even before we turn to the encyclopaedia to check. Wind-resistant plants are apt to be small leaved, often with a

Hippophae rhamnoides *is a plant for exposed sites and especially suited to seaside areas.*

shiny cuticle (protective outer 'skin') and tight in growth making symmetrical hummocks. Big flaccid leaves would be torn easily and the plant ruined. (An interesting exception, though of little practical value in gardens in these cool temperate islands of ours, is bananas and certain palms, whose great leaves permit tearing in one plane to reduce wind damage. Veins run parallel to the splits so that the leaves' functions are unimpaired.)

Certain areas of the world are particularly productive of plants for exposed sites. These include New Zealand, maritime California (the Monterey Peninsula provides a splendid pine, *Pinus radiata*, and the well-known *Cupressus macrocarpa*) and often the Mediterranean. As many desirable species from these areas lack full frost-hardiness it is as well that a great advantage of many exposed sites is their excellent frost drainage. We are all used to the meteorological forecasts of 'frost tonight in sheltered areas'. The windy garden does not harbour cold air: it generously passes it on to the protected valley below.

Cultivation

But such sites do call for techniques of cultivation, as well as specialised plants, which cannot be avoided. The most important law which should be woven into a sampler to hang above the desk or writ large in neon above the garden-shed door is PLANT SMALL. Impatience is the devil's greatest temptation to the keen gardener (he seldom has time for the more colourful of the deadly sins). But plants must be enabled to develop a robust root system to

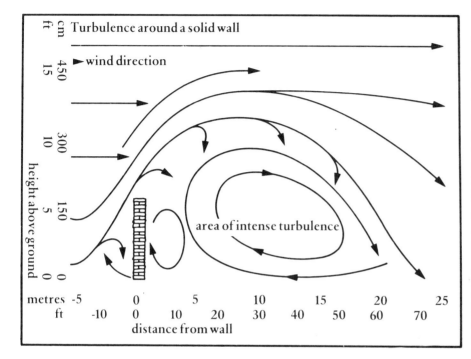

Turbulence around a solid wall

► wind direction

area of intense turbulence

height above ground

cm / ft
450 / 15
300 / 10
150 / 5
0 / 0

metres -5 0 5 10 15 20 25
ft -10 0 10 20 30 40 50 60 70
distance from wall

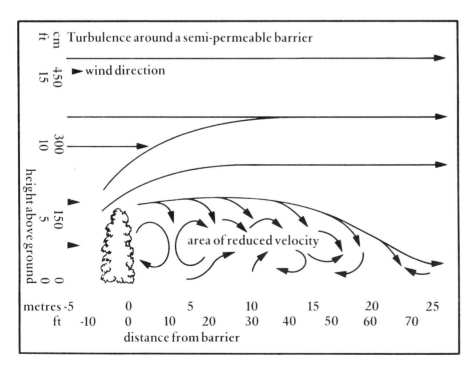

Turbulence around a semi-permeable barrier

► wind direction

area of reduced velocity

height above ground

cm / ft
450 / 15
300 / 10
150 / 5
0 / 0

metres -5 0 5 10 15 20 25
ft -10 0 10 20 30 40 50 60 70
distance from barrier

support and anchor the top. Holm oak, Corsican and Monterey pines should go in as one- or at the most two-year-old seedlings only a foot or so high. Started like this they will take full maritime exposure for a couple of centuries, and as they grow a second line of defence of smaller plants can be added. One or two things with naturally dense and heavy rootballs can be planted bigger. These include *Griselinia littoralis* for mild areas or *Rhododendron ponticum* where it is colder – but only on acid soils.

Wind Protection
Little gardens cannot take, nor do they generally need, tree-sized shelter belts – though it is well to remember that holm oak, for instance, can be kept low by

Much careful research work has been done on the effects of wind movement on cars and aeroplanes and their design reflects this – the current wedge-shape of motor cars is an example. Observant gardeners do not need research to tell them that the effect on plants is equally dramatic and that some, over evolutionary time, have made many design adaptions to enable them to succeed in windy situations. The wind tortured trees seen on our uplands and coasts show the species that have the strength to grow in unsuitable situations but without really adapting to them.

The diagrams indicate the advantages and disadvantages of solid barriers in the garden as wind shields. In full exposure the strong wall by itself causes more problems than it solves. A combination of both types, carefully sited, is ideal.

clipping – it is shrub or hedge help that is vital. In the south and west a number of relatively frost-tender evergreens are unsurpassed: *Senecio rotundifolius*, *Griselinia littoralis* and *Olearia traversii*. These will make a dense 3 m (10ft) hedge even when there is nothing between them and America. In rather colder areas *Escallonia macrantha*, *Lonicera yunnanensis* and *Cotoneaster lacteus* can take over. Fine British natives such as sea buckthorn (*Hippophae rhamnoides*) or gorse (*Ulex europaeus*), the double form *U.e. plenus* is best for gardens, should not be neglected.

Obviously a new garden can be greatly helped by some non-plant shelter material. Good walls and fences are of inestimable value but it must be remembered that really solid barriers can create their own problems as wind sweeps round the end or funnels through any gap. Hedges filter and tame it, avoiding draughts. A possible alternative on the Cornish pattern might be more often tried. They create a stone hedge there, which is really a wide, double wall filled with soil with a hedge planted on the top. This gives height more quickly and the problem of the soil-robbing roots of shelter plants using up a lot of space is to some extent contained.

Not until wind protection has been obtained is it worth planting the more usual shrubs and herbaceous plants, if they are not to be blown out of the ground and the owner go mad with frustration. When it becomes possible, however, this is the time really to explore the range of plants which not only accept but enjoy the position. Its virtues may be in the south or west aspect and relative freedom from frosts. Clean air is also an expected plus. This is the point to visit local gardens to notice how well, for example, all the lovely New Zealand hebes or the fuchsias do amongst shrubs and what a wide number of South African bulbous plants such as amaryllis, nerines and watsonias relish the position. Permutations are never ending.

Maintenance in an exposed site is an added worry. While planting really small will reduce the need for staking, this can never be entirely avoided. Without it a sudden eddy can drag a plant from its bed like a badly drawn cork. Stakes should be adequate and *lasting*; so often in a couple of years the plant is supporting the stake. Once the planting hole has been taken out, tree stakes should be put in before the tree itself, to avoid root damage. Then firm the plant before actually doing the tying. Always after a bad gale go round the staked plants to look for broken supports and chafed bark. It is amazing, too, how rapid trunk growth of, say, a eucalyptus can be ruined within a summer season by overtight ties. Should a plant blow over (and again eucalyptus are particularly prone to this) it is of no use just to jack the thing up and hope for the best. At least half the top must be cut off to reduce resistance. Such rapidly growing plants may need an annual reduction of head to keep top and root in balance.

By concentrating first on the development of a living windshield of tolerant trees and shrubs, many fine gardens have been made in the most unpromising situations up and down our coasts. Inverewe in north-west Scotland is a prime example with its famous collections of frost-tender plants from all over the world and of plants which demand wind protection in a potentially gale-ridden site. Here are seen primulas and Himalayan poppies in the lee of rhododendrons.

The Shady Garden

A SHADY GARDEN IS NOT THE ultimate disaster that many people think it to be. Indeed the phrase may describe anything between a small town patch which literally gets only a gleam of sun in the height of summer and one in which quite a lot of sun is obtained, but where it comes at the wrong time and in the wrong place. A first clear statement should be made: this is that the most completely sunless spot can be enlivened and beautified by plants, for there are many species whose whole evolutionary development has led them to colonise successfully such an ecological niche. In the wild this is likely to be on the floor of thick forest (indeed the reason why so many well-known house plants succeed in dark rooms is that they are from equally dark jungles) or at the bottom of rocky gorges. But if their other needs are met – of moisture, nutrients and an acceptable temperature – they will not recognise a dark city area as anything different.

Shade Tolerant Shrubs

Because of the usually small space involved this situation is not a problem. Walls should be whitened to reflect as much light as possible and an emphasis put upon plants whose effect is similar. Evergreens should be chosen with glossy, highly reflective leaves. Camellias hollies, aucubas and many others have this attribute, whereas yews and other conifers with duller foliage should be avoided.

Similarly, variegated leaves have a lightening effect: *Elaeagnus pungens*, *Fatsia japonica*, hollies again and *Euonymus fortunei* while excellent and shade tolerant in their normal green manifestations also have forms whose leaves are striped with gold or edged with white. For small gardens such variegated plants are particularly useful as the reduction of green photosynthetic leaf area, which variegation naturally entails, does reduce vigour. Watch must be kept for all-green 'reverting' shoots which should be removed at source.

All the shrubs so far mentioned are possible tub or raised-bed plants. Camellias lauded in several sections of this book are especially useful in the latter situations. So long as acid soil is available and adequate water given throughout the year, a dark courtyard can be set aflame for three months in spring with their exotic flowers.

Spring Bulbs

There are less good seasonal plants for dark spots than one would wish. A spring display is not difficult if the emphasis is put upon bulbs and polyanthus and if it is fully realised that they will need annual replacement. Planted in October or November, narcissus, hyacinths and tulips all have their flowers fully formed inside the bulb. The spring

Three plants for shade; on the left are hostas. H. sieboldiana has near-blue leaves, H. fortunei 'Aurea' is soft gold, while H. ventricosa 'Variegata' is edged with white. All have spikes of cool mauve flowers. On the right is a hardy geranium of which several species flower even in dry shade. The brightness of variegated Euonymus fortunei frames the grouping.

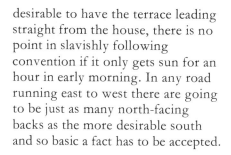

will bring them out and a splendid array can be obtained through careful choice of varieties from February to early June. Go to specialist catalogues for these as the local shop seldom carries a large enough range. But sun and warmth is necessary if they are to build up flower buds for the following year and this is why it is seldom worth leaving them in in really shady spots. Crocuses, by the way, are no use here because they only give of their full beauty by opening in full sun.

Summer annuals are apt to become very leggy in shade and produce leaf at the expense of flower. Therefore avoid choosing plants known to thrive in sun such

Few summer annuals really flower well in shade. Recent advances in breeding weather-tolerant busy lizzies, however, have made glowing colours possible in the darkest courtyard corner. Go to the seed lists for 'White Cloud' or F$_1$ hybrids such as 'Roter Herold' a fine dwarf red with bronze foliage. Put out in June they will, with plenty of food and water, flower until the frosts of autumn.

as pelargoniums (geraniums so called), gazanias and most other 'daisies'. Good are the new impatiens hybrids (Busy Lizzie) and even petunias can thrive.

The Larger Garden

Problems of the bigger garden with excess shade are both simpler and, in some cases, worse. Situations of deep tree shade, with the tree roots having just as wide if not a greater spread as has its leafy top, are areas of dry shade as well. Irrigation obviously helps but the tree is going to benefit the most.

Where, however, space permits a certain amount of flexibility the basic design of the garden must be geared to the availability of sun. Orientation of paths and vistas may not be able to follow the obvious lines from doors and windows because those ways may not lead to the sun. If the sunniest spot is where the dustbins normally live then they must be made to realise that they are occupying a space far beyond their situation in life.

Similarly, while it is highly desirable to have the terrace leading straight from the house, there is no point in slavishly following convention if it only gets sun for an hour in early morning. In any road running east to west there are going to be just as many north-facing backs as the more desirable south and so basic a fact has to be accepted.

Advantages

All is not gloom; there are real advantages. Interesting shade-loving plants can be brought right up to the house – hellebores and bergenia for winter and early-spring interest; primulas and lily of the valley can follow while the summer is a mass of cranesbill (geraniums – true ones) hostas and a host of others which a plantsman in a hot garden would give his eye-teeth for.

Another great advantage of a north-facing house aspect is that, because plants in flower always look towards the sun, it follows that once beyond the immediate shade of the house flowers will be facing south and hence the viewer from the windows. This is a considerable pleasure. Beyond this, in a garden where both deep shade and sun exist, dramatic effects can be contrived where plants can be high-lighted by the sun yet seen against the darker background.

While, therefore, a juxtaposition of shade and sun enlivens a garden and is highly desirable, where shade is preponderant it is not wise to just go ahead as if full sun was a gardening birthright. It has already been indicated that there are numbers of splendid evergreen shrubs which will take full shade, very many others will enjoy partial shade and often their flowering time is lengthened by it. But certain groups of plants or coveted garden features are best avoided.

What to Plant

As regards groups of plants, the great majority of Mediterranean shrubs and shrublets become

The shady garden offers the opportunity for growing a range of exciting plants.

Above *A corner of a courtyard catches an hour or two of late sun in summer. It is planted with big leaved moisture-lovers. Delicate epimedium overhangs the brick, while the whole is lightened with ornamental grasses.*

Right *The leaning tree almost shades the water – waterlilies would not open without the sun. All around are moisture and shade lovers completely covering the ground. Such a garden is not easy to plant but increasing knowledge of plants and their ways makes garden pictures like this possible.*

atypical, even if they grow at all, in the shade. Many of these are the invaluable scented herbs – rosemary, sages, lavenders, savory – and their flowering associates – cistus and santolinas. Sadly in shade flowering is reduced, growth becomes lax and much of their piquant fragrance is lost. Much better is to accept defeat here and concentrate on things which will do well. The cool greenness of a shady place is enhanced by non-flowering plants and many ferns, notably *Dryopteris felix-mas*, *Polypodium vulgare* and *Polystichum*

setiferum will take dry shade with impunity so long as the soil has a reasonable amount of humus. With a little natural moisture the range of lovely ferns increases dramatically and they associate beautifully with meconopsis (Himalayan poppies), candelabra primulas and a host of lovely goodies. Graham Stuart Thomas' splendid 'Perennial Garden Plants' must take on recommendations from here (see Bibliography).

Features

Other areas of specialist interest which the shady gardener (no disrespect intended) will have to avoid are rock gardens and pools, at least in the conventional sense. Alpine plants are evolutionarily adapted to extremely high-light levels, just as the Mediterranean herbs are in their different environment. They must, therefore, be exchanged for small plants which are basically woodlanders. Many of these insist upon an acid soil and hence are admirable for a peat garden. Here limestone rocks must be avoided and porous sandstone used for supporting walls. In moist conditions peat blocks are admirable through which a range of exciting little plants can grow. However, they shrink and curl if allowed to dry out. A trickling rill winding through this sort of woodland is both aesthetically and cultivationally desirable. But open water in shade is seldom anything but redolent of gloom, and if the water is tree shaded decaying leaves build up a broth which is inimical to fish and aquatic plants alike. Surprisingly a tiny trickle fountain in a dark courtyard is not so. It usually develops a surrounding growth of algae and mosses of a brilliant veridian green encouraged by its tiny moist microclimate. Any other way in which the minutiae of a shaded area can be ameliorated will help towards its potential as a place for growing plants.

Garden for a Young Family

GARDENS ARE FOR PEOPLE, AND THIS is apt to mean for young people as well. Children are not, as so many adults seem to think, completely incompatible with a good garden. To choose not to plan or garden carefully 'until the children are bigger' is taking an apparently easy way out. In fact, it is not easy: it means that permanent plants are missing several years of growth by late planting. It also means that children grow up with an atmosphere of 'it doesn't matter' to the garden as a whole and may never develop any attitude of care to plants that are not their own. In this situation the garden is at risk for a couple of decades. Much better to cater for children from the beginning for the mutual benefit of all concerned.

Discipline
Children from a very early age are able to accept that 'this is yours' and 'this is mine', though adults cannot expect children not to be somewhat proprietorial towards the garden in general and treat it as such. Not long ago my then two-and-a-half-year-old son beat the heads off a couple of dozen fine scarlet fosteriana tulips just as they were coming out. He explained 'me not like that colour'. White ones were untouched so that although my anger came very near the surface, there was no alternative but to accept the value-judgment as valid, although the child's reaction to it was extreme! The point is that even young children, hardly beyond the toddler stage, do notice their garden surroundings and react to them.

In many cases behaviour will fulfil expectations. As with the house where scribbling on the wall is unacceptable, if other members of the family care for the garden so too, in general, will the young. This is not to encourage fussy parental 'garden proudness', merely to indicate that, to quote the old hymn 'beneath his heaven, there's room for all'.

With young children, that is under five years old, it is desirable for a mother's peace of mind that the play area should be in sight or at least in earshot of the kitchen window. This means, most probably, a part of the family's important sitting-out area. There is no point in tucking the children's bit away in a shady corner – they won't use it and will inevitably overflow where you don't want them.

Sand and Water
The things especially enjoyed by this age group are sand and water play. Both provide endless opportunity for creative and imaginative play and these lead to development of coordination and manipulative skills. Modern knowledge of child development has given us clear insight that provision of interesting facilities for

An imaginative climbing frame combined with a slide. This is suitable (with early supervision) for ages from 3 to 10 and beyond. At this stage the door and different levels makes it adaptable as a fort to resist invaders or a house for a dolls' tea party. It is sited on sand or grass in a paving surround.

pre-school children at home is not a luxury.

Sandpits need to be big enough for children to experience something of reality in the activities they go in for. Tidy little sand-boxes are more suitable for the cat. Yet it is not unreasonable to expect a certain tidiness if this is a part of the terrace. However, sand will get out from the containers. Raised sandpits are bound to be messy. Much better that sand distributed during a play session can be swept from the flat into the hole. Pits constructed in an area of rectangular paving are simplicity itself. The ideal is to have a pit within a pit of a size which is not out of scale with the area available and is arranged on the module of the paving stones 75 cm × 150 cm (2½ ft × 5 ft) is a good size for the sandpit itself and will accommodate four reasonably civilised children without undue warfare. Thirty centimetres (a foot) of sand whose top is 15 cm (6 in) below paving level is about right. The double pit effect will provide two terraces for sitting space. It does not matter if sand gets wet (you cannot build anything with sand that flows like a television commercial for table salt) but a cover is desirable. It should be narrowly slatted if the area is a part of the terrace that is used often, otherwise a frame with chicken wire to prevent fouling by animals is sufficient.

Nearby can be sited a low table – a flagstone cemented to a block of stone is suitable – where a bath of water can be put out for water play. No matter that sand and water will be brought to each other – better than soil and water any day. Sunken water for this age is a mistake and a potential danger, but the thought that the sandpit might be sub- sequently converted into an ornamental pool can be considered when the pit is being planned. For remember, children do, eventually, grow up.

Growing up

After a time they wish to be able to play away from mother's view from the kitchen sink and having become more responsible, a children's area out of sight is soon desired by everybody. Play becomes more adventurous and this is a time for swings, climbing frames, tree houses or whatever facilities can be provided. The more desirable from a child's point of view these are, the better for the rest of the garden. This does not necessarily mean great expense and sophistication. Children are enormously resourceful; a large packing case can be as exciting as the smartest Wendy house. This area is best grassed and should be sown with a hard wearing mixture. In order that it will have settled down to take the wear desired of it, forward planning is most desirable.

Seclusion, of course, can be provided quickly with a row of runner beans or Jerusalem arti- chokes, but if time permits or an old garden is being brought into use, something in the way of jungle

A sensibly sized sandpit with a sitting ledge around. If this can be planned as part of the grown-up's terrace children can be easily supervised when very young. Later, when it has ceased to be used, such a hole, linking with the paving module, easily becomes a flower bed or, with a butyl lining made-to- measure, a pool.

effects will be appreciated. To achieve this plant bamboos, large-leaved butterbur and similar wild-garden plants.

There seems little to be said constructively about ball games in relatively small gardens. They will be encouraged by putting virtually everything to grass, restricted or banned accordingly to the attitudes of the parents and convenience of facilities elsewhere. We all know that while it is good to have our children playing safely and near they will naturally gravitate to the best spots for the current craze: provide too much of *le jardin sportif* and the whole neighbourhood will use it. And you will have to give them tea as well!

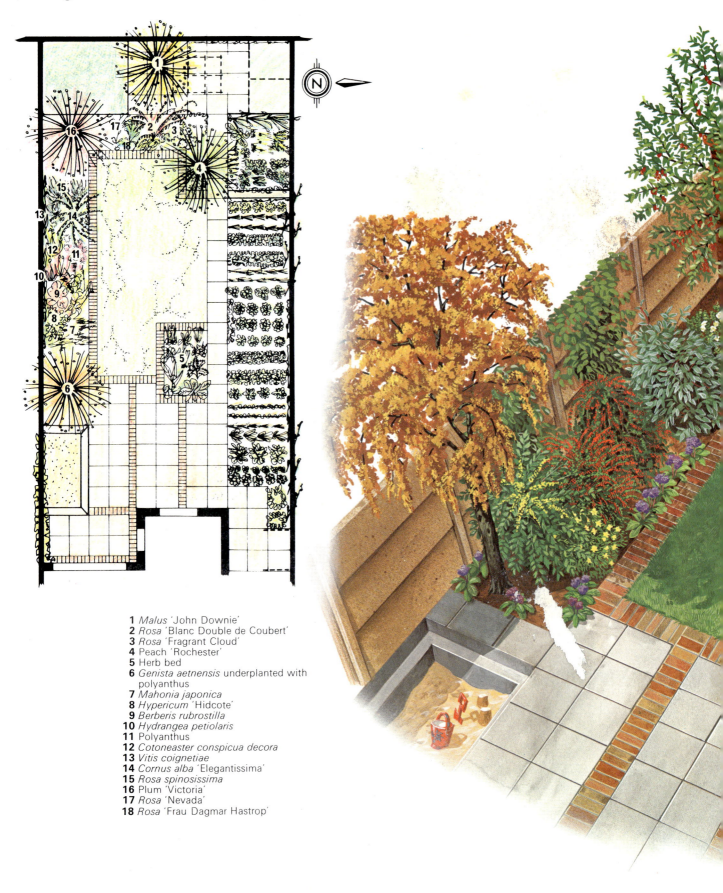

1 *Malus* 'John Downie'
2 *Rosa* 'Blanc Double de Coubert'
3 *Rosa* 'Fragrant Cloud'
4 Peach 'Rochester'
5 Herb bed
6 *Genista aetnensis* underplanted with polyanthus
7 *Mahonia japonica*
8 *Hypericum* 'Hidcote'
9 *Berberis rubrostilla*
10 *Hydrangea petiolaris*
11 Polyanthus
12 *Cotoneaster conspicua decora*
13 *Vitis coignetiae*
14 *Cornus alba* 'Elegantissima'
15 *Rosa spinosissima*
16 Plum 'Victoria'
17 *Rosa* 'Nevada'
18 *Rosa* 'Frau Dagmar Hastrop'

Gardening for Children

If parents are interested in gardening so, most likely, will their children be – at least until an age of rebellion. Young children enjoy helping to sow or harvest vegetables. Boys as well as girls like to be able to pick flowers, and should be shown how to do so and what is permissible from an early age. Young children's help in the garden does need to be on their own terms; nothing is likely to put them off for good more than jobs that are obvious chores (later no doubt this is valid). The children's own terms are often best met by having their own individual plots, when they want it and for as long as they want it. Quick maturing annuals, especially edible ones, are desirable and there is no reason why a couple of square yards against the path in the vegetable plot shouldn't develop into a miniature cottage garden as cornflowers and radishes, peas and petunias compete for space. If this does become a keen pleasure it is a good idea for children to cut up seed lists (after use) to make scrap books showing the things they are about to sow and grow.

It is possible in a small space to accommodate most family activities and still have a garden of interest. Conventional ball games are not easily provided for but a negative attitude does not help. Better to offer the relatively controlled alternative of 'tethered tennis' with the ball on an elastic string, clock golf or, after a continental holiday has sown the seed, French boules.

The big terrace is designed to permit family meals and a sandpit. At the bottom of the garden the shed can either be father's province for tools and odd jobs or a children's Wendy house adjacent to the climbing frame. The built-in compost bins may well be used as part of the local assault course but are essential if the garden is also to provide good fruit and vegetables.

For Retired Gardeners

MUCH IS MADE NOWADAYS OF redundancy, early retirement and even with normal retirement at the age of 60 or 65. There is, we are told the problem of increased leisure. This may well be a concern of great sociological significance but it is not, surely, one which affects gardeners of even moderate enthusiasm. Many people, rightly, look upon retirement as the moment to get on with things they have never had time to do before.

Without the rigid timetable of workday commuting and, when the children were young, no less demanding weekend excursions, a garden can at last be the oasis of peace and gentle pleasures. The suggestion is that there is now more time for gardening. Yet there is no point in actually making work for the sake of it. Better then is it to

realise that the usual seasonal tasks – the techniques of soil preparation for the kitchen garden or the tidying of the herbaceous plants at the end of autumn – can be fitted in parallel with the vagaries of the weather and the condition of the soil. With more time available the recommendations mentioned in an earlier section of this book of working *with* rather than against the elements become more practically possible.

It is this convenience which can make retirement gardening positively easier than before. And it is just as well because one is less physically robust at 65 than at 40. In spite of that it is wise to work towards a garden whose design does actually save effort, because a time

will come when the more demanding tasks cease to be much of a pleasure. 'Working towards' indicates a time scale of some length and one where the retirement gardening continues. Moving to a new home, with a bare uncultivated plot can be a daunting experience indeed.

The older the garden usually means that areas of mature shrubs or of shade beneath trees can be left without much effort being expended upon them if time or health does not permit. For as one gets older one presumably wants to spend time on the really profitable and the fully pleasurable. In spite of the apparent prospect of a vista of deliciously un-programmed days and years stretching ahead, one frequently hears retired people say that they have never been so busy in their lives.

What is usually possible is to keep up the small, specialist cares which go with cultivation of a certain group of plants, whether it be Japanese chrysanthemums or species cyclamen. The day-to-day observation coupled with what practical help can be abstracted from the specialist texts frequently turn the interested amateur, who did what he could at weekends, to the acknowledged expert to whom others come for advice.

The Gardener's Den
It becomes necessary yet again to ask the question, what do I want?

The gardener's den should be a place where the gardener can get away to brew up a cup of coffee while he sows his seeds and keeps his garden diary.

And for whom? One aspect seems particularly important; as the garden is likely to be used more frequently, the convenience of its parts and its buildings becomes vital. A garden shed which can only hold tools and the lawn mower is not big enough for a potting bench and for storing compost ingredients and such. Wherever possible it is very desirable for the keen retired gardener (however loving and supportive his wife) to have his own 'den' – a well-lit, heated workshop/potting shed with water laid on. The classic story comes to mind of a wife looking forward to her husband's retirement but saying 'I married him for better or for worse – but not for lunch'. People do need to be able to get on with their own ploys and in this context, while much concern is rightly given to the change in life-style of the man, that of the woman no longer alone for much of the day is equally cause for consideration.

Any such potting shed, then, needs something of a time and motion study done upon it with convenience and ease of work the keynotes. It is usual for peat and sand to be kept under the bench. Might it not be sensible to have help to get a bale of peat at a higher level to avoid continual bending. Everyone can work out his own needs in this line: doors should be wide enough to take a wheelbarrow or truck, racks for tools should be placed at the most convenient spot and height. Any greenhouse space (see page 154) is best incorporated into this same complex, both for ease and for saving in heat. Potting shed and plant house therefore interrelate.

Labour-saving Techniques
In the open garden the emphasis needs to be upon common sense and labour saving: more interrelationships here. Large areas of kitchen garden for the production of food to feed a family is no longer so

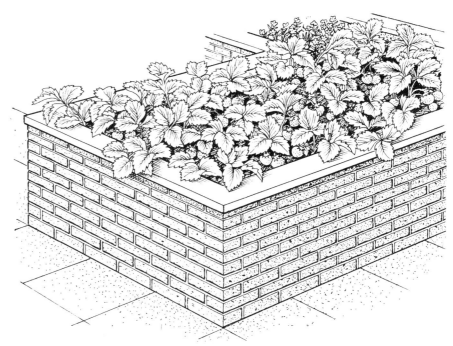

Raised beds of this type both add to the architectural 'bones' of a garden and make cultivation easy; a wide coping at sitting height helps considerably.

necessary. What is needed are small quantities throughout the year, especially of those vegetables which quickly lose quality in the shops. It is very easy to maintain a twelve-month supply of salads – so long as a daily lettuce is not essential – with chicory, headed cabbage, winter radish, land cress and celery to give the winter supply. Small amounts of a number of things is wise. To facilitate this a vegetable plot can be divided into narrow strips, 1.23 m (4 ft) wide, with 60-cm (2-ft) paving paths between. Such beds will take three rows 45 cm (18 in) apart very nicely, or a central row of peas with a lower catch crop of lettuce, turnip or radish on each side. Maintenance is easy and dry access for this and for harvesting is always there. On heavy clay soils it is worth raising the beds by a few inches, edging with upright paving, concrete blocks or treated timber held in place with pegs: the improved drainage and soil structure will halve the physical effort needed. Note too

should be taken of the 'no-digging' school of gardening. With sufficient organic material available for mulching this has a lot to offer.

For the larger garden, if owners have not already become machine minded, retirement is the time to do it. Extravagant it may be, but a small sit-on mini-tractor is invaluable. It acts as a luxury wheelbarrow, will cut both rough grass and lawn grass – all permitting a standard of cultivation that would be exhausting by other means. Suitable machinery for small-scale ploughing and subsequent arable cultivation of vegetable plots is not easy to find. Some cultivators are too light, others impossibly heavy to manoeuvre. Nonetheless, if one wishes to deal with relatively large areas and has some 'feel' for the internal combustion engine (there is nothing more useless than motorised equipment that does not work, and nothing more expensive than continual visits from the garage) serious consideration coupled with effective demonstrations from the retailers should be given to this aspect of garden aid.

On a smaller scale it is narrow minded not to keep reasonably abreast of improvements in herbicides and pest control. It is

undesirable to turn the plot into a
small-scale chemical warfare unit
but if, for instance, the choice is
between scrapping the asparagus
bed because weeding on the knees is
just not on, or using a couple of
applications of weedkiller, the latter
would seem to be more sensible.
Similarly, with aphids being their
usual pestilential selves on the roses,
it is reasonable to use a systemic
insecticide very infrequently rather
than having to rush out weekly with
the rhubarb-leaf water, however
temporarily effective. One cannot,
blindly, accept all the optimistic
blandishments of the chemical
firms – but progress is made and
should be accepted with gratitude.

Gardening for the Disabled
Emphasis so far in this section has
been upon enjoying the retirement
garden and reducing and making
labour more logical. However,
there are occasions when sadly the
problem is more serious. People
just cannot bend down or are quite
unable to get about without aid.
Yet gardening still provides a major
pleasure. If it does the idea of giving
it up entirely is a quite unnecessary
wrench. Possibilities are several:
a terrace area adjoining the house,
with no steps in between, can have
all beds raised to table-top height
with a width of about 1.25 m (4ft).
They can be used for ornamental
plants and are referred to in the
chapter on 'Rock Gardens', but
there is no reason why they could
not be used for vegetables or
strawberries, brought on early with
cloches.

Certainly losing fresh vegetables
would be a major tragedy if
gardening became impossible. It
would be worth exploring the
possibility of letting a neighbour
with no or too little garden take
over an otherwise unused kitchen
garden plot in return for a few
vegetables. Merely to know it was
not going to rack and ruin would
give much reward.

The basic rectangle is here made easy to maintain while still offering the possibility of growing a wide range of plants. The raised beds are made of the same brick which also edges the single step. It is highly desirable to make such a change in level easily seen and negotiable. The flags are laid regularly upon sand; omitting the mortar filling in places will permit seedling plants to soften the effect—it is surprising how well good garden plants do in a tiny crack. It is important that the fountain spray does not reach the waterlilies.

1 Apple 'Ellison's Orange'
2 *Chaenomeles speciosa*
3 Summer bedding plants
4 *Cistus* 'Silver Pink'
5 *Magnolia liliiflora nigra*
6 Spring bulbs
7 *Clematis macropetala* 'Markham's Pink'
8 *Ceanothus rigidus*
9 *Eccremocarpus scaber*
10 *Trachelospermum jasminoides*
11 *Jasminum officinale* 'Affine'
12 *Lonicera sempervirens*
13 *Olearia scilloniensis*
14 *Ruta* 'Jackman's Blue'
15 *Helichrysum serotinum*
16 *Rosmarinus* 'Seven Seas'
17 *Buddleia fallowiana*

Gardens are for Plants

IN OUR CULTURE THERE IS NO DOUBT that the title of this section is a perfectly acceptable truism. Where Napoleon described the English as a nation of shopkeepers, any latter-day Boney might more correctly say a nation of gardeners. But it would not be a term of abuse. Everybody (or nearly everybody) does garden, even in the most unpromising of situations. Books or articles describing noteworthy gardens seldom bring their gaze down to places of less than an acre or so, or move far from favoured sites. Yet splendid gardens exist in dark town-house areas, 3 m (10 ft) below pavement level, and even of tower-block balconies as any open-eyed wanderer can see.

What makes these places, and the great Sissinghursts, Hidcotes and Inverewes, is their plants in all the diversity and delight which the plant kingdom can show. That gardens are for plants, if not an English invention, is clearly part of the folk tradition of these islands, from cottage window sills upward. And this folk tradition refined by William Robinson and Gertrude Jekyll from the 1870's has produced, by development and evolution, the best sort of gardens we have today. It is not a universal tradition: cerebral refinements in Japan or Italy, for instance, produced very different results. Although had their equivalent of a cottage mode been worked upon, a closer resemblance might have been the outcome.

Diversity of Plant Material
One reason for the development of native plantsmanship is the climate of north-west Europe. Indeed climate is too definite a word – weather is much better. It may not be possible to plan a picnic or a barbecue in the garden a fortnight in advance and be sure of sun on the day. But there will be no lack of variation with alternate optimism and black despair (where on earth shall we put all those people?) in the intervening time.

It is this extraordinary diversity of weather, usually without extremes of summer heat or winter cold which permits our gardens to grow, with suitable care, plants from all over the world. Hardly a country from the Arctic to the subtropics is unrepresented. A walk round the garden with this in mind provides a dizzying, Jules Verne-like experience: Michaelmas daisies and golden rod from America, passion flowers from Brazil, *Berberis darwinii* from Chile, New Zealand flax, Australian mimosa, camellias and cherries from Japan, cotoneasters from the Himalayas, viburnum from China, Indian horse chestnut, tulips from Iran and all the plants that have been brought back from Asia Minor and southern Europe since the Crusades and before.

The diversity amongst the trees, shrubs, climbers, herbaceous plants, bulbs, alpines and aquatics which will grow in the open garden is both a continuing delight and one which is utterly daunting. Which of the fifty plus ceanothus to choose, or of the literally hundreds of rhododendrons?

Magnolia stellata

Cotoneaster horizontalis

Choice from such diversity poses many problems. How to know what exists is followed by how to know what is available. While the local garden centre may be admirable for a bale of peat and a few roses, it is unwise to depend upon what happens to be there the day you call. This is not knocking garden centres, many provide a most valuable service, but obviously like any other general store, a garden centre can only stock that which is likely to sell and sell relatively quickly. And unlike those splendid ironmongers which can be found in the country, where everything is eventually to be found in one of the back sheds where it has been lying for years, plants do not store; they require continual attention until they are sold.

Learning About Plants

There is no answer to this problem

Caltha palustris plena

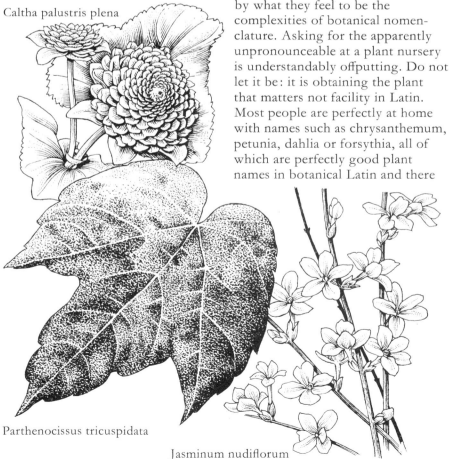

Parthenocissus tricuspidata

Jasminum nudiflorum

other than to encourage the intending garden improver to get to know his plants, which are the paints of the palette of the garden-planner. Books full of bright ideas and ravishing descriptions and pictures can only be a part, and a lesser part, of this. It is essential to see plants growing. Fortunately garden-visiting has become something of a national sport in recent years and each year sees more owners opening their gardens on behalf of some charity or other. It is a danger if one lives in a cold part of Yorkshire, say, to lust after the delightful exotics seen while on holiday in Cornwall. Local gardens will give the most help.

Naming plants which are admired but unlabelled is a perpetual problem. Especially people starting their gardening from scratch and with little background knowledge of plants. They are apt to be put off by what they feel to be the complexities of botanical nomenclature. Asking for the apparently unpronounceable at a plant nursery is understandably offputting. Do not let it be: it is obtaining the plant that matters not facility in Latin. Most people are perfectly at home with names such as chrysanthemum, petunia, dahlia or forsythia, all of which are perfectly good plant names in botanical Latin and there

is no reason why the rest should not be equally accepted. Coy cries for 'common' names are unnecessary: much worse is that they can cause confusion and prevent one getting the plant which is really being sought. It is well-known that bluebells in England are very different plants from the bluebells of Scotland. Where good vernacular names exist this is fine, but it is a mistake to coin them for their own sake.

Accepted botanical nomenclature is not a difficult system. Each plant carries a double scientific name, the first is a generic one, its genus (which by analogy can be considered its surname), the second its species (like a christian name). Examples of plant genera are dahlia, prunus, laburnum, and alyssum. Within each genus exist a number of forms, known as species. Each of these is significantly different and has developed these differences in response to a range of habitat conditions over evolutionary time. In order to distinguish between them, specific names are added to the generic ones, giving the dual name.

For example, *Rhododendron mucronulatum*, a small deciduous rosy-purple shrub from hillsides in Japan and Korea, is both linked by its genus to, and distinguished by its specific name from, *Rhododendron sinogrande*, a vast tree-sized species with evergreen leaves almost 1m (3ft) long and football-sized heads of yellow flowers. This one is native to forests in Upper Burma and Yunnan. It does matter, then, to get the name right if one of these plants is wanted for a small back garden.

In addition to the range of species which have been collected in the wild and brought into cultivation many have developed sports, such as variegated shoots which have been taken off and rooted as cuttings, or have been carefully interbred to give an even greater range of forms. Just as our modern

garden peas are very different from the wild Mediterranean plant *Pisum sativum* from which they are derived, so many ornamental plants exist in a range of colour forms or sizes. These variants are known as cultivars: to be sure of getting exactly what you want it will be necessary to ask for, for example, *Buddleia davidii* 'Royal Red' or *B.d.* 'Pink Pearl'. These cultivar names, which are not latinised, are frequently (as here) self explanatory. Latin plant names, too, are often descriptive. *Betula pendula*, the silver birch, definitely tells us something about the plant, as does *Cotoneaster horizontalis*. But they may also be commemorative (Victoria, Forsythia), geographical (*Choisya mexicana*, *Arum italicum*) or merely fanciful. The point is they are names by which it is possible to refer to this one rather than that.

Identifying Plants

To obtain a little facility with this game it is wise to visit good parks or botanic gardens – several university towns have the latter associated with a School of Botany. Here things are labelled and from this point it is possible to move forward.

Having identified the admired plant or having made up the list of desiderata the next problem is obtaining them. It must be accepted that really rare plants may just not be available anywhere but the lists of sources in the back of this book may help. There are specialist nurseries for trees and shrubs, for herbaceous plants, for bulbs and for alpines. Some specialise even further and grow a huge range of cultivars of only one or two genera, pelargoniums ('geraniums') or dahlias. There are societies of cyclamen growers, orchid growers or more broadly, keen gardeners in general. All these assist in promoting interest in plants and making them more available. There really seems no excuse for a dull garden!

Effective associations of plants building up individual garden pictures are one of the most important facets of good garden design. Felicitous combinations of leaf shape and colours, size and shape of plants and, of course, flowers as well are not difficult to arrange if once the plants are known and their requirements understood. Here (left) with a backdrop of grey Artemesia arborescens *(this is rather tender and likes wall protection) are white regal lilies and statuesque spikes of acanthus. The pink and orange alstroemerias (Peruvian lilies) are highly effective garden flowers and make admirable cut floral arrangements as well.*

The Non-Gardener's Garden

THERE IS, AS HAS ALREADY BEEN stated, no particular moral goodness in gardening. Good gardeners may be nicer (so other gardeners are given to think) than other people, but they are not necessarily better. Yet there is, whether we like it or not, something of a stigma attached to nettles round the door and a patch of mud instead of a lawn. This is particularly easily attached in areas of close housing; comparison being proverbially odious.

It can presumably be assumed that the non-gardener, in fact, is a perfectly reasonable being who prefers to spend what spare time he has on other pursuits. He may sail, or play sport or lay about with the Sunday papers. He will probably also prefer to have a tidy, agreeable garden around his house (knowing, too, in his more practical moments,

that this is not unrelated to its value should he decide finally to move). The concern, therefore, of this section is with the reduction of personal effort. A conventional method is to employ what is euphemistically known as a jobbing gardener. Yet while not wishing to exploit anyone offering his services in this way, it should be accepted that the wages paid out are often to people, no doubt worthy enough, who know less about the subject than the non-gardener himself. Local help with grass mowing or wood chopping is fine, but unqualified strangers should be kept away from living plants.

It was suggested in this book at the outset, that the two questions 'What have I got?' and 'What do I want?' should be answered. The non-gardener often wants some of the things that quite keen gardeners want – a warm sunny terrace with the privacy and protection plants can give. But he also stipulates that

little time is available for the cultivation side of things. However, he will accept that, if a garden is to exist at all, some effort, albeit small, is necessary. He should, therefore, try to decide which of the perennial chores are least acceptable or most time-consuming. Some non-gardeners are perfectly happy striding behind a lawn mower and thinking deep thoughts the while: others will consider it the most foolish occupation.

If the garden area is small there is little problem on that score. It will be wise to extend the terrace area, though not to the point that the garden ends up as a concrete wilderness. The more paving there is, the more important is the associated planting to soften and humanise the hard surface. Important, too, is to vary the hard

A simple but effective arrangement, with oriental overtones, of paving and stones softened with a small bamboo or tall grass. Here the central feature is an old mill stone; many other superannuated artifacts would be equally suitable.

surfacing so that its textures, picking up and throwing back light, relieve visual boredom which a single material can provoke. Such materials are discussed later – cobbles and sets where walking is not necessary, bricks to edge or frame areas of rolled gravel or paving, diversity of shapes in paving, variation in colour (but used with great care). Loose gravel in contained areas and shapes is of great value; texture is good, it is labour-saving yet permitting occasional plants to emerge from it. Gravel up to their necks prevents most weed development.

Labour-saving Gardening

Labour-saving planting for the non-gardener relates, paradoxically, to that of the enthusiastic plantsman. Whereas the latter is avid to use every inch of his soil, the former is equally keen to cover his and get it out of sight. In general, the effects may not be far different.

In the context of labour saving the right plant species are vital and this is, of course, where the essential disparity begins. Here plants are wanted which, ideally, quickly reach their allotted span and having done so stay that size and look good for years to come. Sadly this is not a frequent phenomenon; quick-growing trees are likely to keep at it – hence the inadvisability of willows and poplars and free growing Leyland cypress in small gardens – while quick-growing shrubs are often short lived. Nonetheless it is in the context of woody plants that most of the interest will come.

The effect to be aimed at is of areas of inanimate material for access or use giving way to areas of evergreen ground-hugging plants from which shrubs and trees emerge. Thus ivy in green or variegated forms – the latter help to lighten a dark understorey of leaves – makes marvellous ground cover. Height is given by groups of shrubs on a

Herbaceous borders are certainly not, in their traditional sense, labour saving. Yet some of their plants in other contexts can be. Peonies are an example, not needing division for ten years or more and going on from strength to strength. The species and older hybrids need no staking either.

60 per cent to 40 per cent evergreen to deciduous ratio. These can be chosen to give particular interest at times when the garden is likely to be most in use.

The reason why ground-cover plants are successful at keeping down weeds is obviously the thickness and speed of growth. It will be necessary therefore to cut back or thin these out should they start to clamber up into the shrubs. Lamiastrum, a lovely variegated dead-nettle, is particularly aggressive and will just flow over small shrubs making them look like children's toys left under an eiderdown. Less strong ground cover will permit daffodils to be underplanted and give spring interest and Spanish bluebells can follow on.

As it is frequent cultivation of ground which is anathema, annual bedding plants are definitely to be avoided, unless it is a tub by the front door or on the terrace. Many herbaceous perennials, too, need lifting and dividing every two or three years. Some, however, can coexist with ground cover and shrubs very happily for years. Peonies are an excellent example. Their leaves are good from the time they unfold in early spring to September when they often colour up well. The flowers – singles, doubles or anemone centred – are just lovely.

Fruit and vegetables

These are best left out of the discussion except to commend those which get on with whatever they produce without the need for spraying, pruning and other horticultural fuss. A fine possibility is the mulberry: this is a splendid specimen tree for all but the smallest gardens because of its late leafing; fruit will not come for ten or more years but it is well worth waiting for: splendid for jam, sorbets, freezing or just eating – greedily and very ripe. Other good trouble-free trees for conserves are quince and ornamental crab apples such as 'John Downie' or 'Dartmouth'. The stone fruits, too, plums, gages, damsons or a peach in a warm back garden are worthwhile (avoid the front garden for anything which will attract boys *and* birds). They flower beautifully in spring and in some years will produce a good crop. If only a single tree is to be planted consult a list for self-fertile varieties.

The easiest vegetables are the long-lived perennials such as rhubarb or Jerusalem artichokes. Even an asparagus plot need not be much bother if worked with a herbicide regime.

The simplest (though not the cheapest) thing to do with a behind-the-house strip is to lay it all down to concrete. It has been done; but that is not a garden. Here, for the non-gardener is a valid and attractive alternative. Basically the whole area is covered with 8cm (3in) of gravel over ground which has been cultivated and gently firmed. By scraping back the stones, plants can be put in to give colour, interest and privacy and these are chosen for their labour-saving attributes. Careful use of herbicides will prevent weeds from showing their ugly heads.

 1 *Picea omorika*
 2 *Yucca filimentosa*
 3 *Festuca ovina glauca*
 4 *Erica lusitanica*
 5 *Erica carnea* 'Springwood' and
   E.c. 'Vivellii'
 6 *Genista cinerea*
 7 *Kniphofia caulescens*
 8 *Erica australis* 'Mr Robert'
 9 *Erica vagans*
10 *Cordyline australis*
11 *Azara microphylla*
12 *Aralia elata* 'Variegata'
13 *Arundinaria nitida*
14 *Camellia* 'Lady Clare'
15 *Camellia* 'Francis Hanger'
16 *Camellia* 'J. C. Williams'
14, 15, 16, underplanted with
   Vinca minor
17 *Erica mediterranea*
18 *Calluna vulgaris* 'Searlei' and *C.v.*
   'Searlei Rubra'
19 *Phormium tenax*
20 *Daboecia cantabrica* and
   D.c. alba
21 *Erica arborea alpina*
22 *Betula pendula*

Country Gardens

For non-gardeners a country garden offers similar problems and more besides. Especially as so often it is a weekend retreat, meant for rest rather than two days of toil. Near to the house, where hard surfacing is both required and looks appropriate, the earlier part of this section is valid. Where there are areas of grass or orchard more thoughts are needed. Accepting that formal lawn maintenance is just not on, it is seldom that no heed can be taken of it at all. A reasonable *modus vivendi* is to aim at a cut once or twice a year with a motorised scythe for the main areas. Mid to late June is suitable for the first and this gives time for naturalised bulbs to go down for their summer rest and for the exquisite cow parsley to have flowered. If, however, further wild plants of interest exist, that cut may have to be delayed. The hay will need to be raked off. A second cut may be necessary in areas of high rainfall as late as October if a bulb-inhibiting tangle is not to develop by next spring.

Such areas can be of very great beauty. If it is desirable to bring them into the garden scene, because of nearness to the house, they should be framed in a band of formally mown grass. This need only be of one or two mower's widths. Similarly, if views are obtained into the country a mown swathe 1.2 to 2m (5 to 6ft) in width should take the eye and potentially the walker into it. This makes clear the necessary movement of house, terrace, informal garden and country to develop with apparent naturalness. That which appears the most natural is often the product of the most careful artifice.

The Plantsman's Garden

PLANTSMAN IS USUALLY A TERM given to an enthusiast for a definite range of plants, sometimes not worrying too much how his garden looks as a whole. It is the plants that matter, he will say. And of course, for him, this is so. Dahlias like dinner plates, chrysanthemums in rows, each bloom a miracle of incurved petals hidden in a paper bag lest moth, dust, earwig or sun corrupt before the day of the local flower show dawns. This book is not intended for that enviable kind

A plantsman's garden knows no bounds. It can be large or very small. Here in and around a terracotta strawberry pot is a specialist collection of houseleeks (semper-vivums) which keep their interesting shape all the year, yet change colour somewhat with the seasons.

of specialist of whom it is said, like the legendary Jowett of Balliol 'What I don't know isn't knowledge'.

The plantsman's garden of this section is concerned with collections of plants grown for their own sake yet in conditions and associations which suit and set them off best. They are seen both as individuals and as part of the garden scene. This sort of gardening knows no bounds and has no limits of space. On the one side there are vast areas such as Exbury in Hampshire with its near-definitive collection of rhododendrons, on the other tiny courtyards with equally near-definitive collections of houseleeks or snowdrops. The level of success is shown by the standards of

cultivation and the choice of specialism in relation to the garden and the conditions of soil and climate it enjoys or suffers.

Societies

Not that heavy clay will put off the keen herb grower, or a bleak garden the camellia enthusiast, if they are determined to succeed. It is so often seen to be the case that where the prudent would stop the real aficionado goes on and succeeds. Perhaps people no longer pamper their plants as in the days of the 17th-century tulipomania but the temptation is there, as the catalogues appear every autumn and spring. Fortunately enthusiasts beget enthusiasts and mutual exchange is usually possible, especially if, as with many plants, a specialist society exists (what in other spheres might be called a fan-club).

Such societies, of course, also provide information upon the needs of the chosen range of plants, which will supplement the necessarily less specific information available from the conventional text books. Following this, whole plots turned into alpine landscapes, impeccably grown fruit or Japanese scenes filled with bonsai can be found.

Plant Communities

A plantsman's garden has, however, another connotation. Here taste is more catholic and what merges is a successful application of ideas discussed in the section 'What have you got?' Such gardeners will work with their soil and conditions to build a garden full of interest at all times of the year. Understanding of

the needs of the plants, beyond that of their basic nutrition, is necessary here. With this comes knowledge and further enthusiasm – a splendid self-fulfilling situation.

A basic fact concerning the plant kingdom has first to be accepted. This is that every plant species is an organism in its own right perfectly adapted for the conditions extant in its habitat. Take the well-known *Narcissus tazetta*, for example, flowering at Christmas on its Cretan hillside in poor eroded soil, surrounded by spiny broom, Jerusalem sage and developing seedlings of *Chrysanthemum coronarium* and asparagus pea. These five species, and others with them, have evolved to the point of success in that habitat – the classic Mediterranean sea-level climate of soft, moist winters and searing summers. And they have combined to form a balanced plant community. Each has developed its own answers to the problems of soil and climate: the narcissus by winter flowering and then, after seed setting, complete retreat to the bulb underground for the months of drought and heat. The chrysanthemum does it by having a seed-to-seed life cycle of only four to five months. The shrubs manage by reducing their water-losing leaf area to a minimum (often none) or protecting their leaves with woolly coverings. For all, the point of their efforts and adaptations is the successful annual flowering and subsequent fruiting. All is geared towards the continuation of the species.

A similar story, less over simplified because obviously many factors have been omitted, can be told of every plant community in the world, whether of high alpines on a Himalayan scree, our local flowers of a meadow or wood or the extraordinary complexity of an Amazonian jungle. All this accounts for the incredible diversity and fascination of the plant kingdom.

The successful plantsman, then,

will accept that his plants, even in cultivation, are getting on with their own life cycles to the best of their ability for themselves, not for him as such. He will also realise that most plant species, although individuals, do not live in isolation in the wild. They are part of a community such as that just described. Under trees there are shrubs, under the shrubs smaller woody plants and herbaceous subjects, whilst in the shade and protection which these provide, ferns and other lower plants find their niche and capitalise upon it. A natural community is a full one – the old truism of nature abhorring a vacuum is patently obvious here. It is most unusual for bare soil to remain uncolonised for long. Soil grows plants; that, as far as plants are concerned, is why it is there.

In the garden, then, the best effect is one of barely controlled luxuriance. The idea of the natural plant community should be kept in mind for any mixed border. In the light shade of *Cercidiphyllum japonicum* some lacecap hydrangeas

might be grown. At their foot are hostas, round which are a host of spring bulbs to use the period when all the others are leafless. They commandeer the light, get on with their display and then, like the players in a prologue, disappear from the stage when the main curtain goes up.

This sort of plant community is, of course, likely to be completely artificial. The plants may originate from a number of widely dispersed continents or countries, they may never meet in the wild. Yet if the ecological niche to which their growth pattern, leaf type and so on show them to belong is considered they will, with the plantsman's help, find a comparable niche in the garden. Knowledge helps the placing; the plant itself shows whether that placing is right.

A plantsman's garden is also recognised by its intelligent use of plants. Species which complement each other and share similar cultivational requirements. Here in the gentle shade of cercidiphyllum are hydrangeas and the broad leaves of hosta.

1 Succulents and cacti plunged out in summer
2 *Yucca whipplei*
3 *Yucca gloriosa* 'Variegata'
4 *Beschorneria yuccoides*
5 *Hedera helix* 'Goldheart'
6 Dwarf bulb bed
7 *Gentiana sino-ornata*
8 *Lithospermum diffusum*
9 *Rhododendron racemosum*
10 *Daboecia polifolia*
11 *Erica lusitanica*
12 *Rhododendron* 'Cilpinense'
13 *Androsace primuloides*
14 *Hypericum olympicum*
15 *Juniperus communis* 'Compressa'
16 *Iris pumila*
17 *Dianthus deltoides*
18 *Aethionema* 'Warley Rose'
19 Nymphaea
20 *Pontederia cordata*
21 Petunias and pelargoniums
22 Moist bed of ferns
23 *Epimedium x rubrum*
24 *Helleborus argutifolius*
25 *Hemerocallis* 'Black Magic'
26 *Euphorbia* 'Fireglow'
27 *Ligularia clivorum* 'Othello'
28 *Schizostylis coccinea*
29 *Thalictrum rochbrunianum*
30 *Veratrum album*

It is perhaps unlikely that so many different habitats for differing plants will be required, for most plantsmen, although having a catholic taste in their admiration of plants, are apt to concentrate and specialise on a relatively small range. But the broader view in quite a small plot is possible and, of course, it might be necessary to arrange for a horticultural Mr. and Mrs. Jack Spratt.

Here, depicted in its early stage, there appear to be an excess of walls and coping. But plants will climb up and tumble over to soften the hard surfaces in a remarkably short space of time. As always building materials in the garden should repeat or complement those used in the house.

This sort of grouping is obviously not possible in all parts of the garden. Some conceptions, such as an herbaceous border, leave out the upper layers, yet the principles hold true. Flag irises are a joy for a month of the year – but what then? Why not add interest to that bit of border with a few of the smaller daffodils, such as 'February Gold' (it's never out until March) and, if the soil does not lie wet, some primulinus gladioli in amongst the iris rhizomes for some high summer blooms.

The plantsman too, will use, not moan about, those apparently difficult spots in the garden. The north wall, the shady border, the low-lying bit of intractable clay at the bottom of the garden all say 'NO' in fluorescent capitals, to whole ranges of plants. But there is always a 'yes', albeit lower-case and black and white, to others.

It could seem that this sort of gardening is unnecessarily laboursome, but such a fear can be refuted. The use of ground cover plants, which stratification naturally implies, means that continual surface cultivation is no longer needed, weeds are less likely to be a problem (so long as the beastly perennials such as couch grass, ground elder and creeping thistle are completely removed first). If the number of species is kept small this sort of planting is really very labour-saving – though this starts to be the subject of the antithesis to this section, and belongs to the chapter which follows.

Herbs in the Garden

THERE IS NO DOUBT THAT HERBS have become of much greater interest in recent years. This is both fortunate and logical. Fortunate because their neglect makes a large number of very attractive plants unavailable (as is often experienced, plants not often grown become even less grown because nurseries rather naturally do not propagate what they cannot sell). Logical because many herbs have dual roles at least and so are particularly useful where space is limited. An initial confusion in nomenclature needs to be cleared up. Botanically a herb is a plant which is herbaceous; a plant which dies down to the ground each year and which is not, therefore, woody.

In the conventional vernacular it means something very different. A herb is a plant which has culinary uses, for flavouring or medicinal applications. By extension aromatic plants and those which have historical reputations or folk uses are commonly included. The range of herbs given this connotation is obviously very wide, going far beyond the herbs which most people can name on the fingers of one

Basil

Dill   Chives

hand – parsley, thyme, sage, mint and marjoram.

Except for the enthusiast (and herb growing is apt to develop into a consuming interest unless kept under strict control) the herbs to be generally recommended are those which can combine their economic uses with visual appeal. There are plenty of these, and, as this book is more concerned with design and the use of plants in gardens, these are the ones to be concentrated upon.

Native Habitat

A large number of aromatic herbs are native to the hot, dry hillsides of the Mediterranean region and it seems likely that their scented, pungent leaves are designed as something of a deterrent to grazing animals – though, as anyone knows who has seen a flock of scraggy Grecian sheep in full champ, and has subsequently had the pleasure of eating a herb-impregnated chop, the deterrent is not very effective. To a gardener that habitat says much of what these plants – sage, rosemary, lavender, savory and many others – require from a cultivational point of view: maximum sunlight and perfect drainage at the root especially in winter. They are so happy in the thin chalky or lime-stone soils which are the despair of many gardeners that it is sensible to capitalise upon them there.

Herb Garden

Conventionally a herb garden is an enclosed area of formal beds and, as a conception, is still a valid and a charming one. Many of the shrubby herbs mentioned above as well as thyme, curry plant and several species of santolina make admirable dwarf hedges. All are easy to propagate and cuttings pushed into sandy soil under a cloche in August are usually rooted enough to line out, a foot apart, as a hedge the following late spring. The space thus enclosed can either be filled with a selection of less striking, but nonetheless interesting, herbs or filled solid with one of the low shrubs as ground cover in the manner of a 17th-century parterre. Purple sage and variegated sage are both magnificent plants for this: the only trouble is that the difficult decision has annually to be made whether to let the purple form flower or not. The flower, a sea of colour, is splendid but comes at the expense of the equally splendid young foliage. Two plants, or two beds if there is space, provide an answer.

In practice the separate herb garden is not always possible but all of these plants are admirable (given their cultivational needs) edging a terrace lining a path or indeed in bays fronting higher shrubs. On a small scale a very adequate and surprisingly comprehensive herb garden can be made by lifting three or four flagstones from a terrace. The idea can be happily extended to make an easy-maintenance herb bed by laying paving on a chequer-board pattern. Much of the stone is soon covered by the growth of the plants yet access for weeding or gathering the herbs is always easy, even in the wettest weather. Most of the plants spread far out from their original spot. For this same reason they are admirable in raised beds where they will tumble over the edge. On a still smaller scale a window box will hold a surprising amount of herb growth.

If herbs are for use as well as ornament, convenience is important: the window box on the kitchen window sill and the herb bed close to the kitchen door are both desirable, so long as they get sun.

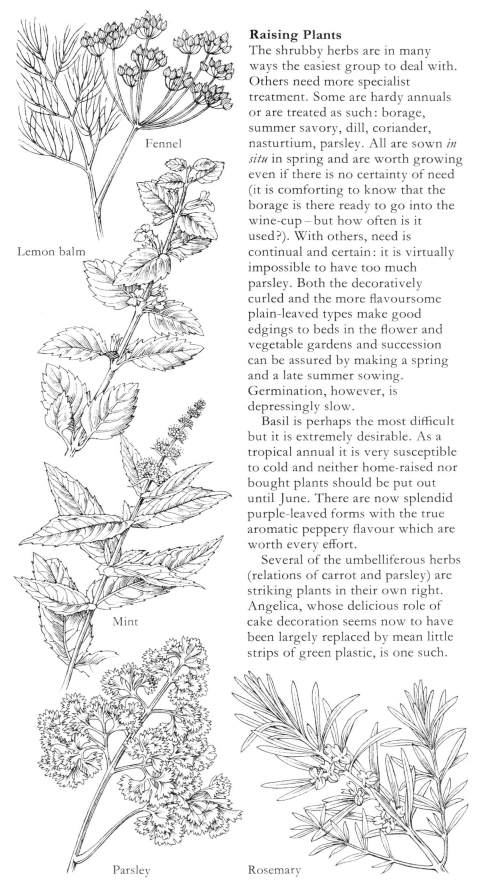

Fennel

Lemon balm

Mint

Parsley

Rosemary

Raising Plants

The shrubby herbs are in many ways the easiest group to deal with. Others need more specialist treatment. Some are hardy annuals or are treated as such: borage, summer savory, dill, coriander, nasturtium, parsley. All are sown *in situ* in spring and are worth growing even if there is no certainty of need (it is comforting to know that the borage is there ready to go into the wine-cup – but how often is it used?). With others, need is continual and certain: it is virtually impossible to have too much parsley. Both the decoratively curled and the more flavoursome plain-leaved types make good edgings to beds in the flower and vegetable gardens and succession can be assured by making a spring and a late summer sowing. Germination, however, is depressingly slow.

Basil is perhaps the most difficult but it is extremely desirable. As a tropical annual it is very susceptible to cold and neither home-raised nor bought plants should be put out until June. There are now splendid purple-leaved forms with the true aromatic peppery flavour which are worth every effort.

Several of the umbelliferous herbs (relations of carrot and parsley) are striking plants in their own right. Angelica, whose delicious role of cake decoration seems now to have been largely replaced by mean little strips of green plastic, is one such.

Its great spherical head of lime-green flowers remains statuesque for weeks and dries beautifully. More delicate are the green and purple fennels, both a mass of filigree leaf throughout summer. These are happy in moist and even shady positions.

Certain herbs need the reverse of encouragement. Unless one is both an addict to its sauce and a glutton for hard work, horseradish is best excluded from all but the biggest gardens. Mints, too, are invasive but essential. They need constant moisture to maintain tender growth and a good way to deal with them is to plant the roots (really rhizomes) in large plastic pots or sleeves. These are then plunged into the ground with the rims just above soil level so that any clandestine running about can be controlled. This method also makes it possible to bring a pot into warmth to get some early growth and a taste of spring ahead of time. Where only a window box is available the variegated apple mint should be grown: it will not provide the same amount of mint shoots but at least it will not swamp the other plants.

Variegation is an attribute of many herbs which adds a further visual dimension to these invaluable plants. Golden marjoram makes splendid little tussocks, but is apt to scorch in full sun. Thymes come in both silver- and golden-edged forms, there is even a variegated horseradish.

In the magnificent National Trust garden of Sissinghurst Castle, created by Victoria Sackville-West and Harold Nicholson, is one of the best herb gardens in the country. Here is a mixture of culinary and old-fashioned medicinal plants grouped for use and ornament. Careful yet unobtrusive staking and gentle clipping over permits this ideal controlled luxuriance. Silver hummocks of santolina and lavender contrast with purple sage; height is given by the apothecary's rose and feathery fennel. Houseleeks adorn the central bowl.

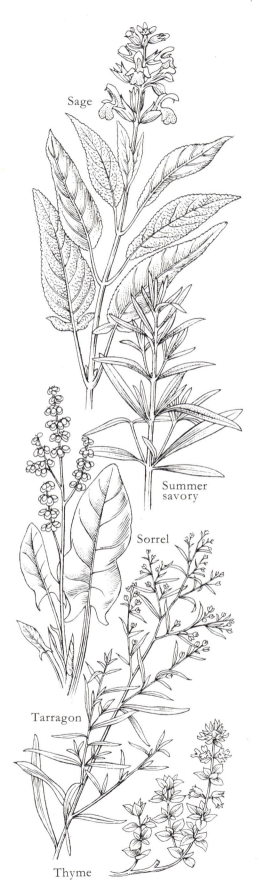

Sage

Summer savory

Sorrel

Tarragon

Thyme

Roses

There must be very few gardens worthy of the name in Western Europe which do not attempt to grow a rose or two. It is this same addiction to roses that still manifests itself in every ex-colonial hill station throughout the tropics. Roses spell home as much now as ever they did in the past. It is sad therefore that the way in which they

Rosa gallica

Rosa 'Fragrant Cloud'

are used in most gardens of the smaller size is so unimaginative. The reason for this, no doubt, is the usually small appreciation, not of the charms of roses – this is a part of our folklore, legend and literature – but of the diversity of types that is available. This diversity has never been so great; it seems a pity not to look beyond the first marvellous 'Peace' that meets the eye.

Hybrid Tea Roses

Discussion of roses is apt to begin with wild species and the early forms and crosses before coming to those most commonly seen and therefore known. In many ways it seems more convenient, if historically illogical, to start with these. We are referring to the bush roses which are more correctly called hybrid teas (HT's). Their ability to leap into leaf and flower within a few months of planting makes them the darlings of the new garden. Flowers are luxuriantly large, of exquisite form, often scented (the dusky, musky fruitiness of 'Fragrant Cloud' on a warm summer evening is a positive incitement to bad behaviour: it compares very favourably with the more highly regarded old-fashioned roses and the flowering season continues from the end of June until the hard frosts come). It is very often possible to pick a few end of season flowers for a Christmas dinner table. The range of colours is remarkable: proof of the hybridists' art, but the brightest are not necessarily the best. Floribunda roses, with crowded heads of usually smaller flowers have similar attributes to HT's.

Using Roses in the Garden

In the heady atmosphere of such a plethora of choice too little attention is paid to the way in which these modern roses are used in the garden scene. Where a garden is enviably big enough to boast a separate, enclosed, rose garden the problems are minimal. In most cases, like the washing line and the proverbial poor, roses are always with us. For it must be admitted that from December until early April conventional rose beds are nothing but a mess of miserable prickly sticks. They need, where possible, to be integrated into the garden so that the months of their disarray are passed over without any thought that the ground could be better used.

Firstly a group or two, each of five plants perhaps, of hybrid teas or floribundas can give summer interest to a mainly spring shrub border. In such a position with tones of green as a backing up, clear bright colours are effective. Groups can also be used with herbaceous plants in conscious combinations of complementary colours; such as the rosy-red 'Rosemary Rose' with *Artemisia* 'Lambrook Silver' or the pale blue flowers of *Salvia haematodes* for instance. Where a bed of roses is required at the end of a terrace, there is again no reason why the bushes should not share the ground. Underplanting with polyanthus and grape hyacinths gives spring interest as does the encouraging of the seedlings of small annuals such as the lovely little 'Johnny Jump Up' violas.

Although the recommendation sounds dangerously purist and

pedantic it really is wise, if the garden is considered as a carefully furnished room, to keep the numbers of varieties to be used very small indeed. A dozen 'Whisky Mac', with their lovely foliage and bronze-orange flowers will look better than a dozen different varieties in the same bed. If this sort of range is wanted for cut flowers, a row in the kitchen garden is the best answer. Standard roses, incidentally, are usually HT varieties budded onto a stock stem some 1.25 m (4ft) high: such a bush on a stick is very difficult to use except perhaps to give height in the centre of large rose beds where it can look well.

Species Roses

Whereas HT's and floribundas are best in the more formal parts of the garden, the wild species from which they are ultimately derived are, not surprisingly, plants for more natural positions. Flowers are inevitably single, with typical dog-rose grace and elegance. With some they are tiny like the little pink threepenny-bit rose R. *farreri persetosa* or the golden R. *ecae*; with others such as R. *rubrifolia* it is leaf and flower in combination that gives the peculiar attraction. Many are aggressively vigorous climbers – small gardens should beware of the lovely Kiftsgate form of R. *filipes* if they wish to have room for any other plant at all.

Indeed, it is to be doubted if it is really wise to plant small courtyard walls with roses at all; invariably they get to the top and hang out their beauties for next door to enjoy. Yet temptation is usually too much. Again, with climbers as with bush roses the range is enormous. Amongst the species R. *bracteata*, evergreen and wickedly armed, has pure white single flowers of great substance, and R. *banksiae*, evergreen yet thornless with yellow or white flowers, are both warm high-wall plants. Others will

scramble through an old apple tree in unpromising conditions.

Many HT's have produced climbing sports and these are admirable for house walls as they flower for such a long period, often opening as early as May in a warm spot. Rambler roses – hybrids especially of the Chinese R. *wichuraiana* – have one glorious season of flower and are best for pergolas or they can be used to tumble down a steep bank.

Old-Fashioned Roses

In recent years the so-called old-fashioned roses have been enjoying a well-deserved renaissance. The current national summer sport of garden visiting has no doubt helped here; for to see these plants billowing about with their spicily scented flowers like Redouté prints come to life at such famous gardens as Sissinghurst, sends admirers rushing for the catalogues immediately they reach home. Early historical types such as the apothecaries' rose (R. *gallica* 'Officinalis' or the striped York and Lancaster (R. *damascena variegata*) never lack fascination but the recurrent flowering (or remontancy) we so take for granted with modern roses is not one of their attributes. That did not come into cultivated roses in Europe until the introduction of R. *chinensis semperflorens* in the early 19th century.

Nonetheless the moss roses and their precursors, of which many old named varieties still exist amongst the Gallicas, Damasks, Albas and Musks, will always have their adherents even for that one short flush of flower. Other groups, notably forms of R. *rugosa*, add to their fine flowering season a long period of ornamental fruits which start to colour in August and, birds willing, hang on for three months or so. Particularly fine is 'Roseriae de l'Hay which has a superb scent and relatively long flowering period.

Other Uses

Uses of roses apart from conventional garden decoration in formal beds has been hinted at. The climbers can be trained up walls and over pergolas or allowed to scramble up a tree. The bushy wild species and their modern shrub counterparts (such as 'Nevada' and 'Uncle Walter') can take normal mixed shrub planting. Many of the old-fashioned varieties have idealised cottage garden use in association with spring bulbs and summer flowers. Even raised beds and window boxes can now contain the little miniatures. Find any site and a rose will follow to fill it – beautifully.

Rosa banksiae

Rosa rugosa

Part 2

Garden Features

What Do You Want?

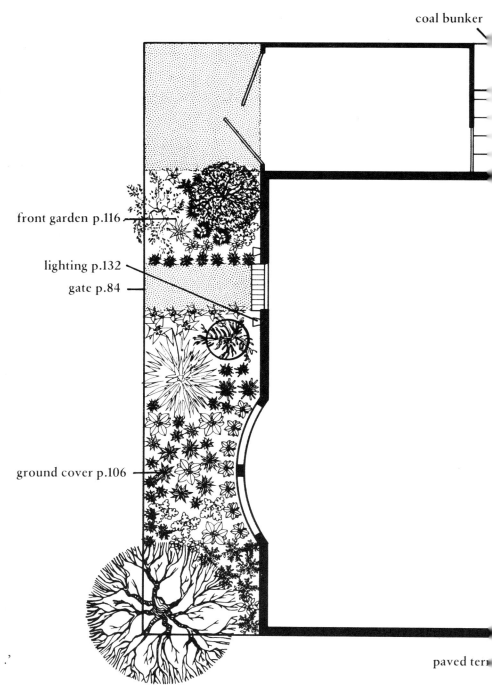

coal bunker

front garden p.116

lighting p.132

gate p.84

ground cover p.106

paved ter

IT HAS BEEN SUGGESTED IN THE previous passages that to make a successful garden you should take a hard and long look at what you have. Look first at the whole site (however small) from all angles. Note especially views from the important windows of the house. Consider the basic shape. List all the plants that you have inherited and get them named. If you do not recognise them then the local park's department will usually help if you take them a flowering or fruiting spray in good condition. Remove as little as possible at first and *never* cut down a tree until you are absolutely certain that it cannot be a part of your design, or you may regret it evermore. It takes decades to grow again anything as mature; and a feeling of maturity is of inestimable value in a garden. This is something which cannot be bought at any price.

In noting what plants are in your own and nearby gardens you will learn something about the soil (see page 20 for soil types and their improvement). You will also have gathered something about the climate of the area through what grows well there. Obviously sheltered plots in warm areas will permit a much more exciting range of plants to grow than will chilly, exposed situations. Extraordinarily, the same dull old plants are seen in both extremes of climate and everywhere else too.

Observe the aspect, the view (if any) and prevailing winds. Maintain a balanced optimism and, like the old Sunday school hymn

'Count your blessings
Count them one by one. . . .'

This is not meant in any way to be a plan to be followed but merely for use as an aide memoire. *It incorporates most of the likely desiderata of a small garden and, in fact, crams in more than could sensibly be used in such a site. But, apart from referring to other parts of the book as a sort of visual index, this is also a way of helping to sort out and choose 'what do I want in my garden?' Draw a site plan to a large scale, list the requirements on individual scraps of paper and shuffle them about from place to place – preferably sitting at a table by the main window overlooking the garden – until a logical and pleasing combination of parts is built up.*

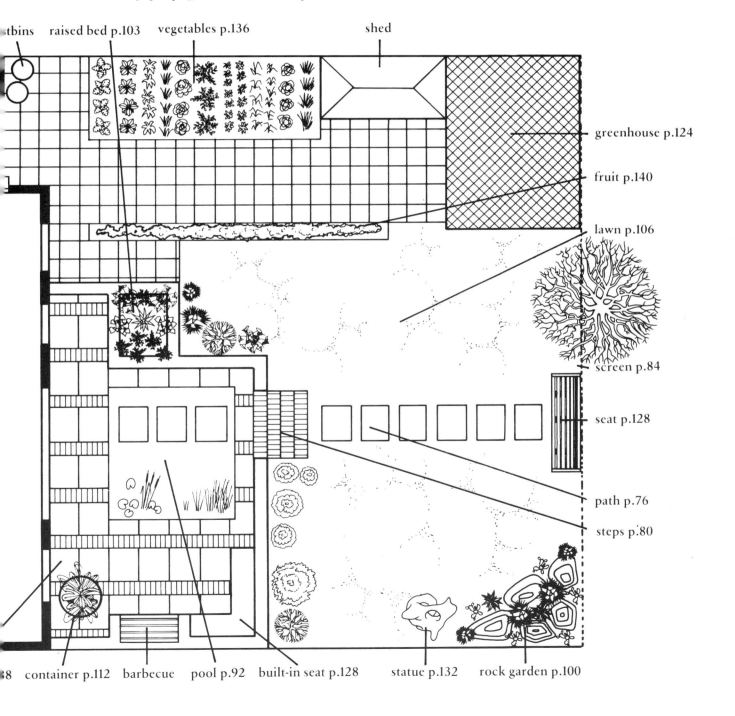

stbins   raised bed p.103   vegetables p.136   shed

greenhouse p.124

fruit p.140

lawn p.106

screen p.84

seat p.128

path p.76

steps p.80

38   container p.112   barbecue   pool p.92   built-in seat p.128   statue p.132   rock garden p.100

Beautiful gardens have been made in the most unpromising sites.

Do try to keep something of a garden book or diary; it will be of enormous help as your garden develops and of absorbing interest in the future as you look back on the successes and even the failures of years past. Noting and listing the plants is important, but is just a preliminary.

'What have I got?' is inevitably and rightly followed by the balancing question: 'What do I want?' Indeed the garden owner, raring to go, may well reverse the order of these questions – but he should not avoid the other. Only the owner and his family can really give answers to the question 'What do I want' and in doing so begin to make their garden personal.

In this book we look at a number of possible answers but the permutations are endless. The plans and comments must be seen as suggestions to be considered in part, rather than blueprints to be used *en bloc*. Do not forget the integral character of the place, which must be worked with.

One central concept, however, does need emphasising; that a garden should be considered as an extension to the house as a place for living in. Because of the vagaries of a northern climate it has taken a long time to be accepted that although many meals and snacks can be taken outside for almost half the year, an idealised Mediterranean life is neither possible nor desirable.

Modern houses are seldom big enough so it seems absurd not to use the space that immediately adjoins the living rooms. No doubt it is more effort to take laden trays outside and bring back the dishes but, apart from the pleasure of being outside on a fine day, one does not have to worry nearly so much about young children dropping crumbs or spilling orange juice. The birds will eat the former and the latter just happily soaks in.

The initial decisions of the design, then, must be based upon the balance of the parts making up the whole. In a very small town garden virtually everything becomes the outdoor room which is already enclosed by walls or other buildings.

In a bigger plot the 'living area' is just a part, hopefully that part leading directly from the indoor living area. A northerly aspect, however, would preclude such convenience.

It is almost inevitable that the rest of the garden is observed or glimpsed from the outdoor room or terrace. But let it be accepted that the outdoor living area is the most important part; the hub of the garden. Other parts of the design depending upon the answers to 'What do I want?', then fall into place much more easily. It is a good area from which to start.

The hub of the garden. Here is an outdoor room furnished with care, not merely with simple no-nonsense tables and chairs but with plants. It leads logically and immediately from the house to invite its frequent use. The opaque corrugated roof makes this more possible than with the usual terrace-outdoor-room-with-the-lid-off, but as the effect is obviously to darken the room inside, such an addition may not often be acceptable. Again, if both sunny and shady aspects can be contrived the use increases, especially for al fresco *meals: many people, while happy to bask in the sun before lunch prefer not to eat in it.*

Paths

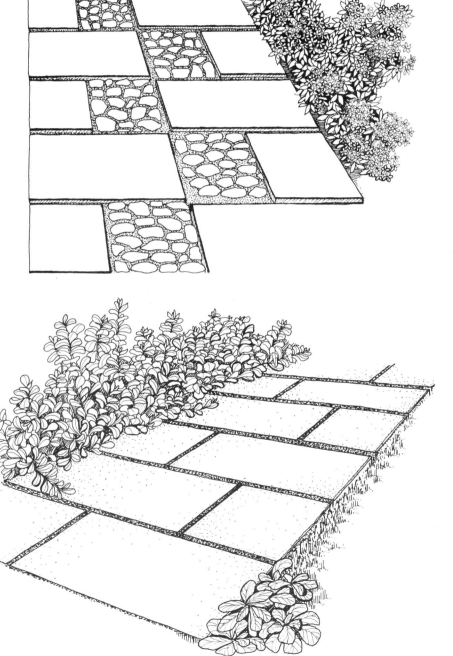

IN THE CONTEXT OF THIS BOOK paths are for people living in 20th-century, westernised society. They are not, as it might often be thought for animals who tidily put one foot in front of the other, or indeed for tribal humans proceeding single file 'Indian style'. It should also not be forgotten how billowing plants narrow a path.

Paths are for convenience, access and, above all, for use. Size, material, position of this facet of the garden compendium is extremely basic to the success of the garden as a whole. For this reason one has to be extraordinarily sure of the initial rightness of any decision to concrete paths, so the dreadful permanence of solid concrete is best avoided at least for some time. Yet hard, dry walking is essential if you are to move around the garden conveniently and with pleasure. Yet again in a small garden it is unlikely that a disproportionate amount of space can be spared for the purely utilitarian service purposes that dry shod walking entails. Several general facts might be kept in mind, the more important of which can then be combined in any specific design.

Paths must clearly go somewhere and go there with dispatch. Those, which, like Coleridge's River Alph '... meander with a mazy motion....' waste space and will with certainty be disregarded by all but drunken users. Even fine straight paths are of no use if there is a quicker or more desirable route between the points ostensibly being serviced. This is often graphically, and lamentably, seen by the paths of winter mud criss-crossed across patches of grass

Four alternatives from a wide range of possibilities. Carefully laid paving by itself with alternate joints gives an entirely different feel from when the joints follow on as in the garden on page 50–51, and for a path is much more satisfactory. A band of paving may also be concentrated by being set in a brick edging or frame. This emphasises the onward-going line. Paths which are not for main service use can be enlivened (though not happily if wheelbarrows are to pass up and down with any frequency) with bands or blocks of cobbles, setts, knapped flints or other, preferably local, material.

in too many housing estates. Notices and fences alike are no permanent barrier to convenience.

Paths also inevitably provide sightlines, or, in more aesthetic terms, vistas. These visual bones of design should look good on the ground and end in something worth looking at. Or, alternatively, if the final point is not good to look at then the main line of the path must be turned. For example, a compost heap is going to need ease of access; it is also apt to be sited at the very end of the garden. A suitable end of vista eye-catcher is sited at the turn, while the utilitarian necessity what-ever-it-is no longer steals the show.

Materials

These of course, are vital if paths are to perform their necessary function. Inevitably the spectre of cost raises its formidable head: *any* solid material is expensive. Hence the right choice for the sort of garden that is being planned is of especial importance. Much of the price nowadays is concerned with delivery costs so that local materials or locally made materials should always be looked at first. Only if they are quite unsuitable should it be necessary to have to look far afield. Anyone planning a garden today can only despair at recommendations seen in books written between the wars when sawn York paving was universally used and cheap to buy. There are still acres of London pavements made with this covetable material.

There is no point either in leaping to the other extreme of cost and deciding that grass paths will have to do. As an access between borders with no traffic other than that of the occasional cultivator or admirer nothing could be better, but wear quickly shows. And as use increases grass paths will need to be disproportionately wide to cope with the flow of people. An added difficulty is on soils which lay wet in winter; here grass paths quickly turn to unacceptable quagmires with need for much subsequent, time-consuming renovation. In small gardens the answer must be 'don't'. However, lawns which are crossed regularly without being main paths can have inset stepping stones.

Practical paths, then, are to be hard paths. If natural stone is impossibly expensive (but *do* examine local possibilities), recourse to concrete slabs is not only necessary but usually very satisfactory indeed. It has advantages too: the slabs are of a definite size and thickness and are thus relatively easy to lay. Quality, of course, varies. Some are variously textured to resemble natural stone more or

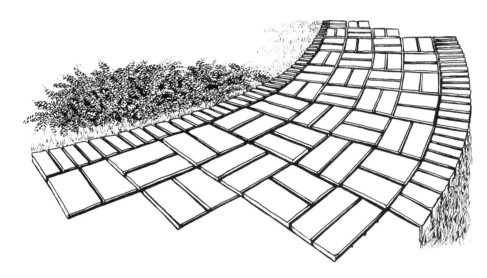

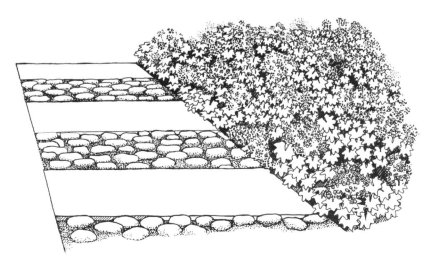

less successfully, but they may be obtained in colours of the rainbow and unfortunately they often are. Unless it is wished to live in the middle of a Neapolitan ice-cream, the quieter colours – and probably no more than two in combination – should be chosen. Choice should be made not merely because colour A is preferred to B (though this is important), but with the consideration of what suits best in the situation. These are discussed at greater length in the section on terraces.

The cheapest slabs are usually simple uncoloured grey concrete ones. These are admirable for service paths: where they are more visible they are immediately brought into another category by being framed in bands or edges of brick setts or small cobbles (the latter at points not walked upon). This same artifice is the only way to make crazy paving acceptable. Certainly broken paving slabs from the local authority dump have their uses – though seldom really as cheap per square metre as might be thought. It is difficult material to use well in any but a country cottage situation.

Stone or concrete slabs are available in sizes that can be combined to enliven the most starkly functional path. Some possible combinations are suggested here: in practice the whole pattern should be drawn out on paper so that the exact number of slabs can be ordered.

Laying a Path
Normally slabs are best laid upon a 5-cm (2-in) layer of firmed sand laid over firmed soil. Subsequent cement grouting where no plant growth is to be permitted in the cracks helps to hold them in place. The likelihood of slight falls or irregularities developing over the years is a small price to pay for the adaptability of paths not irrevocably laid in concrete (and at greater expense).

Levels should be chosen with care. When bounding grass, paths should be marginally lower so that a mower can cut right to the edge with its roller on or overhanging the path. Against cultivated ground, be it flower border or vegetable plot, the path needs to be at permanent soil level. If soil starts to need to be banked up to avoid mess and spillage much space is wasted. Ultimately, small retaining walls could be necessary.

Other materials are possible. Rolled gravel as it weathers gives gentle contrast to plants but is difficult to maintain as the relatively narrow paths of a small garden. It is also suitable as a larger area for general access. Modern weedkillers no longer sentence gravel to be labour intensive as it once was (how many great gardeners have claimed that their careers started on gravel drives with broken dinner knives in their grubby hands?). Gravel's porous surface does permit plants to germinate and grow down and in controlled conditions offers a splendid site for Mediterranean and other plants that like a baking.

In less formal situations walks through flower beds or shrub borders can be made with a sprinkling of pea-gravel or of bark chips. Whatever the level of access needed to any given point, a suitable material can be found, not necessarily at inordinate cost.

It is essential that paths should be wide enough to allow for the billowing effect of plants to soften the hard edges. Such an effect is always delightful but should not impede access; paths are, after all, for use.

Steps

THERE COMES A POINT WITH SLOPING sites where paths can no longer be allowed to drift with the contours. This is particularly the case with hard paths in formal or semi-formal situations. Sloping paving, though no doubt admirable for skate-board activities, looks incongruous and in practice can be positively dangerous in wet or frosty weather. The alternative is to divide areas of flat or nearly-flat path by steps.

As discussed earlier in the section dealing with sloping sites, although such sites are initially more of an effort to lay out successfully, the result is seldom dull. Change of level offers so much potential for varying both plan and planting that where, in an otherwise flat garden, a couple of steps can be contrived, it is invariably worth doing.

As with paths, steps are for access and must be adequate for the task they have to do. It is almost self-evident that they should never be narrower than the path they serve, excluding their supporting piers. And they will most often be wider.

There is no doubt that well-built, well-proportioned steps can be amongst the most beautiful parts of a garden. They catch and take the eye just as they should take (but never catch) the feet. A flight of steps, even in the smallest garden, should never be too steep.

Remember outdoors the sort of steps that lead down to a front 'area', for instance, though probably very similar to those in the house, these appear to be positively vertiginous.

Riser and Tread
These need to be in proportion and in tune with the way we walk and simple recipes for size can be given. Risers should not exceed 13cm (5in) in height to include the thickness of the slab (or whatever) which makes the tread, and this in turn looks well if it slightly overlaps the back of the riser. A 13cm (5in) riser calls for a 38cm (15in) wide tread for comfortable ascent.

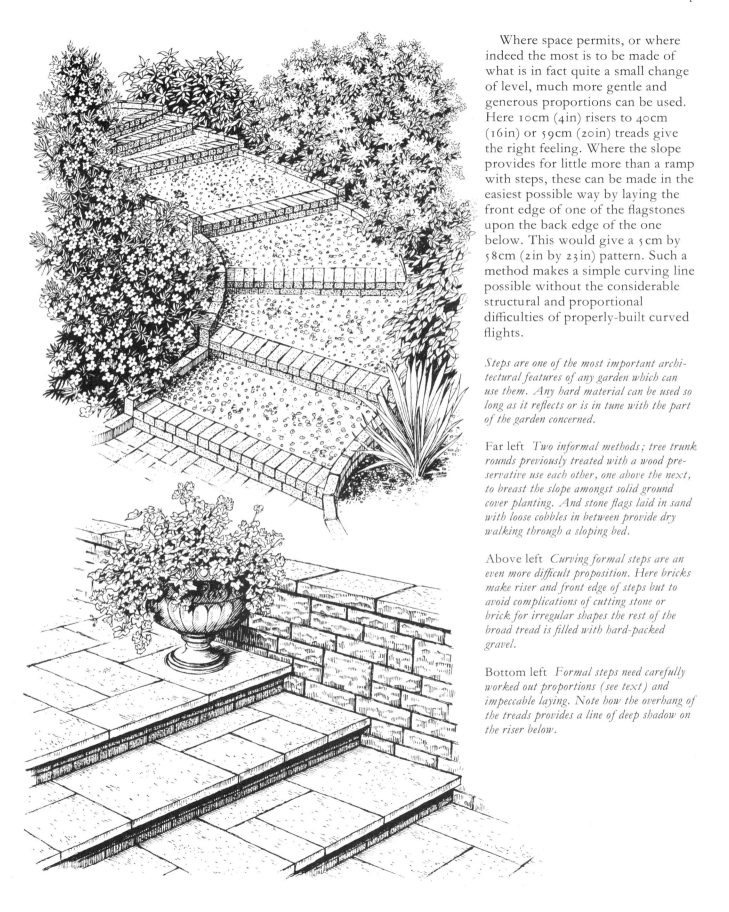

Where space permits, or where indeed the most is to be made of what is in fact quite a small change of level, much more gentle and generous proportions can be used. Here 10cm (4in) risers to 40cm (16in) or 59cm (20in) treads give the right feeling. Where the slope provides for little more than a ramp with steps, these can be made in the easiest possible way by laying the front edge of one of the flagstones upon the back edge of the one below. This would give a 5cm by 58cm (2in by 23in) pattern. Such a method makes a simple curving line possible without the considerable structural and proportional difficulties of properly-built curved flights.

Steps are one of the most important architectural features of any garden which can use them. Any hard material can be used so long as it reflects or is in tune with the part of the garden concerned.

Far left Two informal methods; tree trunk rounds previously treated with a wood preservative use each other, one above the next, to breast the slope amongst solid ground cover planting. And stone flags laid in sand with loose cobbles in between provide dry walking through a sloping bed.

Above left Curving formal steps are an even more difficult proposition. Here bricks make riser and front edge of steps but to avoid complications of cutting stone or brick for irregular shapes the rest of the broad tread is filled with hard-packed gravel.

Bottom left Formal steps need carefully worked out proportions (see text) and impeccable laying. Note how the overhang of the treads provides a line of deep shadow on the riser below.

Above *Simple York stone steps link paving above and below of the same material. The ends of the four-step flight are hidden by the growth of hydrangeas which also, inevitably, screen the retaining wall of the upper terrace. In this way one level flows into another without any feeling of constructional constraint. As always, the planting makes the scene.*

Right *The scale of these steps is considerable using two or three large flags at each level. The width, however, is not constant which permits the softening effect of the planting to obtrude on both sides. At the same time the steps move slowly to the right in such a way as to avoid a full view of the full (and hence visually exhaustive) flight. Construction is simple: the back of each flag supports the front of the next.*

Any feeling of insecurity must be avoided by really efficient bedding of the materials composing steps: here is a case, unlike on the flat, where slightly tipped flagstones or sinking levels are quite unacceptable even in informal situations. To some extent, also, a flight of steps is part of a retaining wall and as such has to withstand stresses greater than any horizontal access path.

Materials

These are as diverse as with path-building. Flat stone paving, natural or simulated is, of course, the obvious material for treads in most formal situations. It can be the same as the terrace or path which is being so linked. Risers can be of the same stone, carefully laid and packed so that the next riser is supported equally at the front and the back. Brick can be incorporated into the scheme with great success;

the brick riser combining well with a stone tread.

As might be imagined, grass steps are almost impossible to maintain yet are still sometimes attempted. In informal positions where stone-built steps might be inappropriate and unnecessary the construction, although not always long-lasting, can be wood. Sawn planks impregnated with a preservative, are pegged in place to make risers with a packed earth tread. This can be surfaced with wood chips, pea-gravel or with pine-needle litter, whichever is most easily available. Good risers can also be made with the requisite lengths of halved larch poles held in place in a similar way. More rugged is a single file flight of tree trunk sections placed one above the other.

Positioning the Steps

In such a situation the planting on the bank that is being ascended, very satisfactorily deals with the naked edge of the steps. With formal terrace steps the decision has to be made whether to cut into the retaining wall or to protrude from it. Both methods, and indeed a third half-and-half alternative, have possibilities and should be considered. Another effective method is to extend the upper level forward for some of the length and arrange the steps to descend at right angles to its front edge from the point where the extension ceases. The retaining wall then conveniently provides a solid backing to one side of the flight. This is one way of dealing with an unavoidably steep flight of steps, where inserting it into a terrace would need difficult excavation and a corridor effect obtained; whilst the opposite apron steps would seem unpleasantly exposed. Wherever and whatever type of steps occur in a garden design they need, because of their inevitable dominance, to be considered at the earlier stage of planning.

Screening: Fences, Gates and Walls

THE CONVENTIONAL IDEA OF THE Englishman's house being his castle, however outdated, dies hard despite the rights of entry given to Income Tax inspectors and policemen. We like to *feel* we have privacy even if we have none. This is exhibited all over the country as people no sooner move into their splendid new picture-windowed houses than they (very naturally) drape them with curtains and blinds in all directions.

Clearly people prefer not to be goldfish. The same attitude is exhibited in the furnishing of gardens. Most people like some seclusion, although they are apt to be considered odd and anti-social if they insist on total visual protection from their boundary walls or fences. Others are satisfied or are expected to be satisfied, by a simple foot-high board to demarcate their limit of possession. Does this really do any good? Or is it just another petty maintenance problem?

As always, there is the need to ask the questions: 'Why fence? Why build a wall? Why have a gate?' For years I lived happily in a house called Blue Gates whose only claim to particular interest was its illogicality of name and some good plants. There were no gates. Fifteen years later I note it still hasn't. Nor are they needed; cows no longer pass up the lane, local louts are no worse than anywhere else. In other words there is little to be kept out – and nothing to be kept in. And what a relief to owner and postman alike, nothing to be opened or shut.

Such an instance does nothing to decry divisions or demarcations,

this is merely to emphasise that there is no law which says that every well-dressed garden should have a gate.

In earlier times walled gardens – some of which have come down to us – had, as walled gardens now, the basic utilitarian virtues of protection from weather and stock. They also provided delightful contrast between the wildness of the countryside and a contrived civilisation inside. Today, an equally delightful contrast is between the busy world and the oasis which a successful

garden must be. Seldom, however, from a financial point of view is it now possible (even were it desirable) to wall in any large area. Hence we return to the questions.

Walls

Walls in the garden have certain clear roles. They protect from wind and weather and from the view of passers-by. They enclose by dividing that area within from whatever 'the rest' may be. They provide a framework of bones upon which the flesh of plants can be very satisfactorily built up. The decision must be made to protect that part where privacy is most demanded. This is most likely to be the terrace

Left *A solid back fence 3 m (10 ft) high supports a seat and canopy.*

Top *A simple wrought-iron gate built into a wall, its arched top relieving the plain facade of brick. While it is always agreeable to be able to look through into a garden, such a gate can permit unpleasant draughts. It would not be too extravagant or expensive to attach a sheet of rigid perspex, or even plate glass, to prevent this.*

Above left *Lath screens change the direction of a path and supported bamboo canes 2 m (6 ft) high are brought out to provide separate planting bays along a boundary fence.*

Above right *Patterns made with laths provide instant height for screening in a new garden.*

or sitting-out area leading directly from the house (where the aspects permits it). Wing walls at right angles to the house will enclose the optimum space. Much more protection is given if walls set at right angles to these main walls are constructed, even if only a metre or so is added. This will provide something of a fourth side to the desirable outdoor living room. Beyond this point the material used is rather less important.

To enclose a living area it is best to continue with the material, or a related one, of which the main building is made. If this is brick the answer is obvious, though expense may be saved by enclosing panels of concrete blocks, or even wood, in a brick framework. Rendered house walls can be carried on with concrete blocks, colour washed in the same way. Small and dark walled gardens, especially in towns, are frequently colour washed to increase the feeling of light: while this is usually a great success, it should not be considered a social inevitability. Well made walls, both old and new, have their own quiet beauty and any added colouring is apt to be irrevocable.

If, as might be expected, plants are to grow on the walls it is sensible to have galvanised vine eyes inserted at 30 cm (1 ft) intervals up the wall and the rows repeated every 3 m (10 ft) of wall so that wires can be easily strung. It seems a pity to make holes in a newly built wall.

The great virtue of walls is their permanence. They weather and age in tune with the house and plants growing upon them can mature too. Nothing is more unfortunate than fine specimens ruined by their support collapsing behind their back.

Fences

Nonetheless other materials exist, and exist in quantity. Of these, wooden-interwoven or lapped panels are the most frequent, being easy to erect, at least apparently so. Their permanence, effectiveness and ultimate economy is enormously enhanced if they can be incorporated into a plan using solid piers or posts and baseboard.

It is vital that any wooden fence is protected in every possible way from rot. Posts entering the ground need an application of hot creosote or proprietary wood preservative. Bottom rails need to be clear of soil. Cappings at the top to shed water will also help. Painting is a wood preservative but the effort of applying primer, two undercoats and a top coat, plus the relatively frequent renewal, makes it a doubtful proposition from an economic point of view. Ineffective painting produces the tatty peeling board fences that are part of too many contemporary housing estate

Walls and fences are to screen the unsightly outside and enclose the agreeable inside. Here a combination of materials in a courtyard fulfils the necessary role while at the same time providing interesting textures against which plants show up well.

Variegated ivy, for example, is dramatic backed by dark boards whereas it would be half lost on the white wall. The height of the screen is disguised by fronting part of it with a raised bed of interesting plants brought to eye level which is in turn softened by further planting at its base. These three layers provide an interesting tiered effect and offer sites to the needs of different plants.

gardens. But if paint is to be used, white is one of the best colours. With a white background plants stand out with clarity and precision. A hopeful green to 'blend with the countryside' is invariably wrong and does no such thing. Similarly, where chain-link fencing is used as an effective, though sadly inelegant, divide, its green form only compounds the trouble.

In some situations the fact that the material used is not permanent and does not pretend to be so is no problem. Wattle hurdles of woven hazel or the more beautiful woven osiers are ideal to give protection while a plant screen is developing. They are available in 2-m (6-ft) lengths in heights from 1 to 2m (3 to 6ft). As with interwoven fencing, wattles last longer if well supported and kept off the ground. Their use is twofold: to provide initial privacy and to give young plants shelter and protection. In really windy situations, especially by the sea, it is only with such help that a first shelter belt can be obtained, in the lee of which more desirable plants can be grown.

Gates

To gate or not to gate and how, is an entirely personal decision. Only a few general points might be made. The height of a gate is best taken as that of the wall or fence of which it must be seen to be a part. There cannot be much point to a gate twice the height of its wall: dogs and paper boys will certainly not bother to open it. Similarly, in a high wall nothing looks better than a wrought iron or solid wooden door with a lintel above. There is a lovely feeling of entering a new world, but to contrive the effect with an arch or other lintel above the line of the wall seldom looks anything but artificial. Again good design combines the logical with the inevitable (at least that which appears inevitable once it has been carried out).

Paved Areas and Decks

In really small gardens, especially in towns, the whole garden may be a paved area, at least that part which is not planted. But regardless of garden size, an area of hard standing against the house has long been a part of garden design in this country since Humphry Repton reintroduced the terrace. This followed after Capability Brown's over-purist approaches had brought grass sward to the very windows of the house. Repton's Regency clientele used the terrace for gentle morning walks. Victorian inheritors embellished it in an Italianate fashion, but took tea in the shade of the deodar on the lawn.

Our simpler, servantless way of life requires different things of the terrace. Sun, shelter and convenience are the particular needs. This room with no roof on, just outside the rest of the house, is the hub of the garden. From here the rest is first seen or glimpsed, from here too it is most likely to be contemplated at length because this is where it is possible to flop down after horticultural exertions elsewhere.

Materials

As an outdoor room a hard floor is vital. One that dries quickly after rain, is good to look at throughout the year because it is so close to the house windows. It should be safe at all times (certain natural stone surfaces can be extremely slippery). It must, too, be complementary to the materials of which the house and enclosing screens are composed. Discussion of some hard materials is made in the section devoted to paths. Many of the same criteria apply, remembering that the nearer the house, the more formal should be the material used. If crazy paving must be used for economy reasons, let it be of panels set into frames of

regular paving or of brick. In this way it is given an acceptable form.

Recently, inspired by an idea from across the Atlantic, slatted wooden decks have become popular as terrace flooring. The great advantage of these is that wood is a more equable material, becoming neither so hot nor so cold as either natural or man-made stone. It is not the economical alternative to stone as it is in more forested countries. A wooden deck can cost as much as stone. Nonetheless if second-hand timber can be obtained, professionally impregnated with preservative, it can compare favourably with more traditional materials and be surprisingly long lasting.

The Terrace

Because of its method of construction, a wooden deck is bound to be slightly higher than the rest of the garden; the step or two down adds to the feeling of a terrace. Whatever the surfacing material, this should be contrived wherever possible, even if it can only be done by excavating the ground in front. Taking 15 cm (6in) of soil from an area and using it as a terrace base will provide a really worthwhile platform. Words of warning unfortunately must be given. If the topsoil is thin it is necessary to skim it off before using the less rich subsoil to increase the terrace level. Topsoil is then replaced or used for raised beds: it is too valuable a material to waste as mere ballast. Again whilst on heavy clay soils a raised terrace is very desirable, an excavated area may become a winter pond and a death sentence for plants or lawn growing in it. Lastly, any terrace raised against the house must take levels of the damp course into account.

Left *Double-glazed doors open onto a raised wooden deck. This is a modern equivalent of the traditional stone-flagged terrace, its balustrade replaced by an extended bench. Formality is emphasised by the clipped hedge in front; a bed of billowing flowers would be an alternative.*

Above *A broad area of paving is broken up into cobbles and*

Below *Softened with luxuriant plant growth.*

Size

Obviously the size of terrace should be in accord with the garden as a whole but there comes a point when reduction to achieve good proportions becomes a nonsense. In such cases it is more reasonable to see all the garden as terrace. Intended use will indicate a desirable size, and it is surprising how much space a few long chairs and a table or two take up. A children's area will require even more. In general the amount of space given to terrace use is too small, when really it should be seen as the centre of the garden. So more than anywhere else in the garden, the planting of the terrace surrounds is vital to a good design.

Aspect

This again depends upon use and it may be found that in order to do the things required more than one such sitting-out area needs to be planned. A south-facing terrace with a straight front is fine for much of the year. But late-evening summer sun moves so far round to the north-west that an arm of the east side, giving an L-shaped effect, will be needed. Positions of existing trees or high walls and buildings may effect the situation.

Shady Areas

While in our climate sun is usually at a premium, there are times when full southern exposure for lunch or tea is too much; hence tree shade on a corner of the lawn becomes a desirable addition to the terrace facilities. If space permits some shade can be provided by a pergola or arbour attached to part of the house or one of the wing walls of the terrace. Such an addition, draped with a fruiting vine or other ornamental climber, adds style to outdoor summer meals.

A north-facing house back will inevitably invalidate much of what is desirable in a house terrace. In such cases only dry access from house to garden is necessary. Close-to-the-house planting, of shade-tolerant species, must be interesting in its own right. From here an inviting path must lead to an enclosed sitting area which gets the sun. Distance is a bore in carrying trays of food and drinks but better this than no opportunity for garden living.

Barbecues

A relatively distant sitting-out area justifies a permanent barbecue spot much more than one right against the house. Generally it seems that a nearby kitchen is a more suitable place for preparing food. But simple portable barbecue equipment (also usable at the seaside or in the country) can be used as a supplement to add that authentic aroma of perfectly good sausages turning into charcoal which fashionable outdoor eating seems to demand.

Two very different areas of paving indicate the possible diversity of material and effect.

Left In a tiny courtyard intelligent use is made of materials chosen from what is easily to hand. Panels of herringbone bricks are framed in regular bonded bricks between formally laid, yet random-sized natural stone flags. Such an arrangement is timeless. It is as suitable for a country terrace as a walled town garden. It can also be added to or subtracted from if design needs change.

Right A more sophisticated bespoke plan uses the blue-flecked yellow London stock bricks for step risers and for walls and raised beds. The railway sleepers which provide the main usable surface, exaggerate the garden's width. Wide gaps avoid a solid effect and provide potential sites for carpeting thymes and chamomile. However garden furniture would need chunky legs or basal bars if spilt drinks were not to be frequent. Such definite lines of paving demand and here get, equally strong planting with hostas, rheums and rodgersias.

Pools

FROM THE EARLIEST TIMES WHEN gardening developed into an art form in the long pre-Christian civilisations of Asia Minor, water has been an integral part of gardens. Pools, fountains, rills, ponds – water in all sizes from a puddle to a lake can be seen in gardens of every age. Of course it is not without significance that the earlier cultures which had gardens, right up until the middle of our own millenium, were in warm climates. Here the sight, sound and even smell of water equated with luxury and a vision of a paradise on earth.

It might be thought that gardening in countries like the ones renowned for their moisture would not be so keen on using water. But this is not so. Almost everyone would like to have a pond in their garden even if only a relatively small proportion of people actually get round to making the effort to get one. For effort there certainly is, though with plenty of reward, both in construction and in subsequent management.

Water in the garden offers several very particular pleasures. The plantsman will at once conjure up visions of delicious exotics thrusting through the surface and marginals clothing the edge. Others will find fascination in fish and other aquatic life. The more contemplative will enjoy that unique watery mirror of the sky which lightens its patch of ground as nothing else can. Still others will rejoice in water movement, slowly flowing or breaking into a scintillating fountain spray.

Introducing Water into the Garden
All these things are possible – not necessarily at great expense. But it is desirable to introduce a couple of warnings at this point. Firstly, that to introduce water successfully artificially into the garden scene is not easy (this lets out the fortunate few who inherit a stream or even an ever-damp ditch). There is more to it than lining a hole with polythene and turning on the tap. Secondly it is just not possible to combine all the desiderata in one spot. Some, indeed, are mutually anti-pathetic. Water lilies, for example, will not succeed in moving water and will languish and die (actually drown) under the spray of a fountain. So, as with other areas of the garden, the question has to be asked: what do I want? And why? From this point a constructive move forward is possible.

It is especially difficult, if not impossible to incorporate an informal pool into a small garden with any hope of making it appear at all natural. The same problem occurs with rock gardens, so often indeed that these two features are apt to be linked. A hole is dug for a pond and the spoil produces an adjacent heap to make a 'rockery'. On a large scale with suitable backing this can be a lovely combination. Even here, however, a difficulty arises with planting the pool. Water-side plants are inevitably large in scale; their evolutionary adaptions to copious moisture makes this so. Hence they tend to dwarf plants (and indeed the site itself) whose own morphological modifications to mountain sides makes them so much smaller. For this reason those irregular glass fibre pond liners (often of repellent brightness – water just does not come that colour except in selected

bays off Capri) are best avoided. They constrict design. Much better to start the other way round: work out the pool's *raison d'être*, its size and shape and *then* find the liner.

Shapes

In asserting the practical difficulties of irregular pools on a small scale, the inevitable corollary must be the recommendation of formal simple shapes. Association with paving and hence the terrace is both practically desirable and visually right. Water always provides a focus of attention and access to it, therefore, needs to be especially convenient. A rectangular or L-shaped pool of only 2 or 3 sqm (6 to 10 sqft) in area provides a splendid link between terrace and lawn. If this is associated, as so often, with a change in level, one of the pool walls may well be at convenient sitting height. This puts the water surface and the water's contents in a position to be the better enjoyed.

Left *A semi-circular tank projects from a higher retaining wall. Such a raised pool with a wide coping at sitting height puts water, plants and fish at an easily enjoyed level.*

Top right *Here the reflective charm of water is used to the full with the formal pool lined with sea-smoothed pebbles.*

Bottom right *Part of a terrace is turned to water. The paving module is continued to make the shape and water level is kept almost to the height of the paving itself.*

Planting

The smaller the area of water, the more restrained the planting must be both of aquatics in the pool and of marginals at the edge. There is little point in having a pool if its surface is so covered with leafy growth that it resembles a perfectly ordinary flower border. Hence it may be only possible to have one of the smallest water lilies such as *Nymphaea tetragona* or *N. × pygmaea helvola* and an aquatic iris, *Iris laevigata variegata* for example, as textural contrast in one corner. Depth of water, again, presents restrictions. Less than 30cm (1ft) makes solid winter freezing a possibility, with resulting death for fish and certain exotic plants as well. This is, of course, perfectly adequate if the role is solely that of sky reflection.

Twice that is about right for most horticultural and aesthetic needs but the danger to young children at least to the age of five must be seen as being omnipresent. Every year toddlers are drowned in small garden pools and to possess unprotected water is to flirt with death. A sensible compromise is to design the children's sandpit of a size and position where it can be converted into a pool when circumstances permit. Such adaptability is mentioned in the section on the Family Garden.

The ownership or prospect of water gardening is apt to lead even the most prosaic into flights of fancy which should be recognised as such. There appear to be inevitable associations in the mind: water, summer, drifting through curtains of cascading foliage, tea in the country and so on, is typical. It leads to a pair of weeping willows being planted, one at each end of a coffin-sized pool. In two years the pool is out of sight and in ten the house disappears as well.

Plants in scale are essential. The weeping effect is better obtained by one of the smaller bamboos:

Arundinaria murieliae for example, or even the corkscrew hazel (*Corylus avellana contorta*) or *Nandina domestica* in a protected spot.

The loveliest pools are those where plant growth exists in each habitat from deep water through the shallow edges to marshy ground. As this is what happens in nature there are numbers of delightful species for every condition. When constructing an area of artificial water where none occurred before the moisture is only within the lining material. If the edge immediately plunges to the full depth of the pool, marginal and bog plants are obviously out unless platforms for pockets of soil or large sunken containers are made.

Construction

Pool construction has gone through something of a revolution of late. Until recently, concrete was the only normal possibility. It is still best in formal situations but the effort needed to construct a garden pool is considerable. Always buy premixed concrete; the amount needed for a minimum of a 15cm (6in) bottom and 10cm (4in) sides is surprisingly large. Reinforcing bars are desirable to key bottom to sides and the whole will have to be done within pre-constructed shuttering which is later removed. A keyword here is permanence, so

Left *Here is water perfectly used, to bring down a piece of the sky and to double the value, by reflection, of the exquisite plants that its presence makes possible.*

Below *Water appeals to another sense, that of hearing as it trickles from rill to pool through carefully placed water-worn limestone rocks. If this is to be an accepted pleasure of the garden's water, it is vital that no hum of a circulating pump is heard. Such obvious artifice dispels every illusion.*

design and position needs great care if time, effort and money are not to have been misplaced. New concrete must be finished with a seal (proprietary materials are available) to prevent exudations poisoning the water for fish and plant life – though three or four changes of water will have the same effect. Incidentally, draining home pools can be difficult. One method combines siphoning the majority of the water by hose-pipe from pool to a main-drainage manhole. The rest is then disposed of through a drain in the pond itself. This is made at building time by inserting a screw-top flagon with its bottom broken into the concrete base. So long as a small soakaway of broken bricks is provided underneath, the residue of any pool emptying is easily lost.

Much easier, though potentially of shorter life, are pools lined with modern, man-made, water-proof materials. Design dangers of fibre glass have already been mentioned. However a rectangular liner with near-vertical sides could be admirable. Shallow dish-shaped ones are difficult to disguise as being anything but what they are: avoid any shape like a diseased kidney.

Thick gauge polythene, treated to resist rapid degeneration from ultra-violet light is doubtless the cheapest method of containing water in the garden. This is laid on a layer of sand in the excavated hole and gradually filled with water, the increasing weight of which causes the membrane exactly to fill the hole. Black is the most satisfactory colour to use. The more definitely

permanent butyl liners, which are made to size, are also most satisfactory in black. These provide a professional finish more easily. 'Finish' is the vital word here. Regardless of the material of pool construction it is essential that its surround is good. This is for access and to mask the edges of the construction material. Water lapping grass is a charming idea in truly natural surroundings of some size; in the garden, however, paving is bound to be the answer, at least fronting the pool. The back could be a retaining wall or even a carefully planted border. Flagstones are laid to overhang the water by some 5 cm (2 in), this produces a shadow which hides the pool's lining. It also gives the pool the impression of cool depths unless it is very shallow. Water in the garden is peculiarly a fact of artifice. Facets of the design should combine to make this artifice appear natural – this is almost impossible – but necessary.

Swimming Pools There is little doubt that of all the desirable garden features a swimming pool is the most difficult to fit satisfactorily into the general garden scene. So much so in fact that keen gardeners have got to be persuaded by their families before, as it might be said, they take the plunge.

If space permits it is wise to consider a swimming pool garden in its own right, separate and separated from the rest of the garden. Seclusion is certainly desirable. If the facilities for swimming are available in the privacy of the garden, it is pleasant to be free from the conventions of dressing demanded by public bathing.

In the case of a young family the warnings offered regarding ornamental pools are no less to be

Swimming pools, with tennis courts are the most difficult things to fit into a garden scheme. Wherever possible the pool should be quite separate from the rest of the garden (also as a safety factor for young children).

Left Prefabricated raised pools are initially cheaper but are very visually intrusive. Here is a way of linking one with a raised deck on one side. Screening plants in front may well be affected (see above) by the water.

Below Here is a simple and satisfactory pool garden in an enclosed courtyard. Walls carry luxuriant planting but the plants are far enough away not to be affected by the water (plants do not like chlorinated water and can demonstrate the fact by dying).

Sufficient space permits desirable furniture and space for lying about.

taken seriously. A swimming pool is bound to be a draw for any young child, but a slip on the edge could mean disaster. For a number of reasons therefore if a door can be shut on the area, so much the better.

Position

It is natural that the sunniest spot should be chosen. Heating methods whether by use of conventional fossil fuels or solar panels are unlikely to be more than supplements to the normal effect of sun on the water and water's natural ability to hold heat reasonably well. Cooling effects are increased in windy situations which add more points to the idea of enclosure. This, provided by fencing or walls well-clothed with suitable plants, can also be helped by the sort of aquatic duvet which is made to be

pulled over a pool to reduce radiant heat loss at night.

In a small garden the number of places which will take a swimming pool are necessarily limited and the effect on neighbours should not be underestimated. The glad summer cries of happy bathers are not always welcome over the fence, and offering an open invitation to swim in order to keep neighbours even marginally sweet is apt to be a bore. Here again thick planting will help to absorb noise.

Obviously very careful professional advice regarding ground levels, availability and disposal of water, types of pool lining, heating methods and cost must be taken. They fall outside the scope of this book which is concerned with the garden as a whole and the visual effect of its parts. It may be that pool-builder and garden planner are not in accord and here as dispassionate a view as possible of the whole and its component parts must be taken.

Above *Fronting a large pavilion is a curved pool. Grass comes close but not too near the edge as an agreeable, though maintenance demanding, alternative to paving.*

Right *Perhaps an ideal situation and admirable planting. Here spiky New Zealand flax and the huge leaves of* Vitis coignetiae *combine with robinia and other background trees to build up a lovely garden scene in its own right. Growth in the front is high enough to conceal the difficult blue of the pool lining but low enough for the elegant bench and the garden house to be glimpsed from a distance, hinting of pleasures to come.*

Use

Actual time spent in the water by the fortunate owners, their families (and the inevitable fair-weather friends who haven't a pool yet) is very short, taken over the year. Here is another reason for not letting it dominate the whole garden. Even in the season more time is spent on the edge thinking about getting in, or in chairs after the exertion of having done so.

A pool then must be part of a terrace/patio complex. Here an ambience can be created to encourage an atmosphere of Mediterranean warmth, however illusory in actual fact. A paving surround must be sufficient that little water splash reaches grass or other plants. They resent chlorine or its modern alternatives. Coy 'his' and 'her' changing rooms are no longer a part of home-swimming pools which have moved into small gardens but if the sitting area can contain a small shelter perhaps fronting the heating unit, where chairs and the inevitable impedimenta of pool maintenance can be kept, all the better.

Shapes

As with a normal terrace and its beds, shapes should be kept simple. Variations on the rectilinear are invariably best; those resembling foetal tadpoles seem more suited to Hollywood and are more difficult to construct. Again terrace planting helps the effect. Containers of brightly cascading summer annuals and those like tobacco plants and petunias which become highly scented on hot evenings are right. Weight and balance is given by the cordyline cabbage palms, New Zealand flax, and other exotic looking plants. Large-leaved climbers on the walls such as *Vitis coignetiae* and *Aristolochia macrophylla* compound the effect. Considered thus, a pool really can add to the pleasures of a garden without detracting from its visual effect.

Rock Gardens

IT IS PROBABLY BEST TO AVOID THE word rockery, for this is apt to encompass all that is unsatisfactory about most small garden efforts in this field. A pile of soil is made – no doubt left over from something else – then scattered at random with bits of stone or even (horror upon horrors) broken concrete. The result is *not* a rock garden and it must be hoped that aubrieta and alyssum spread quickly to hide the hideous heap.

It should be said that a successful rock garden is one of the most difficult garden features to position, to construct and subsequently to maintain. What, then, are the attractions? There are, of course, many. There is the wish to bring into the garden a piece of real, wild, 'natural' countryside; the sort of countryside which is almost of necessity, the most distant and different from the position offered by most small gardens. The natural rock, it is fondly hoped, stretches down deep into the earth to be a part of the truly natural world. Often in the wild such rocky outcrops are crossed by tinkling streamlets, deep pools reflect the clear sky and overhanging ferns. Such places are redolent of holidays and freedom, not the workaday world.

For these very reasons it is inevitable that to recreate such an idyll on a garden scale is virtually impossible. Also, much of the peace and calm of the natural scene comes through the near monochrome effect. A few harebells, a cushion of thyme, a patch of moss – each changing with the seasons – is the only bright colour. The moment we

An indication of the way in which rocks should be laid. It is vital to avoid the purely cosmetic effect of stones dotted about the surface like cherries on a cake. The base of the rocks should not show. Lines of natural stratification should be constant and rocks should lean back slightly to conserve rain, but all at the same angle. The effect to be aimed at is of an area of natural rock which happens to come out of the ground at that fortuitous and fortunate point.

add our rock garden plants, gathered for their spectacular beauty, from mountainous areas all over the world (and often made even brighter by hybridisers) we detract from the 'natural scene'. Yet the other prime reason for building a rock garden is to grow these very plants. The paradox seems hard to avoid, but it is not impossible.

Creating a Rock Garden

A first essential is to know what is wanted – is it the effect of natural rock, or is it the plants that are most important? If it is the former, then the careful siting of, perhaps, only four or five fine, big rocks in an important focal point is what should be attempted. This is really creating sculpture with natural materials, and is only possible in an area where stone is freely available without great expenditure. But it is better kept this way, for rock work in areas where natural stone does not exist cannot fail to appear artificial. It is this obvious cosmetic artificiality that must be avoided if successful garden design is to be achieved.

The Rocks

When used for an architectural or sculptural role rocks must be chosen with great care. Cherish sides which show the effects of natural weathering; try to preserve any moss and lichen that already exist. Plan to hide scars or newly-broken faces which may take a long time to mellow.

Early treatises on rock gardens usually recommended that to give the feeling of natural rocky outcrops, stones should be laid, as if they were icebergs – with much more out of sight than visible. We can no longer afford such extravagance, nor is it necessary. However the basic tenet still holds good: no rock should just sit on the soil surface, its base should be hidden so that it appears to go deep down to parent rock.

The other vital fact to keep in

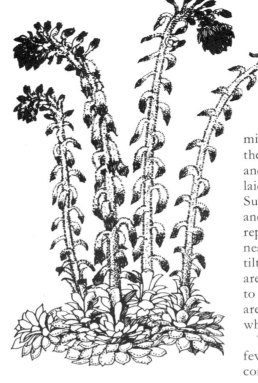

mind is the way the natural lines in the rock go. This is its stratification and indicates how it was originally laid down millions of years ago. Such lines must be carefully followed and the angle chosen must be repeated for the whole outcrop – near to horizontal with a backward tilt is best (rock stratification lines are virtually never vertical). This is to suggest that the few rocks seen are the top of a rocky outcrop from which soil has been eroded.

This type of rock garden needs few plants. Grass or water should come right up to the foot of the rocks and a strongly shaped conifer such as *Juniperus sabina tamariscifolia* or perhaps one of the spurges like *Euphorbia wulfenii* will add to the architectural effect and help to blend it into the rest of the garden scene.

Two of the myriad of lovely plants suitable for rock gardens or a rock bed.

Top Saxifraga grisebachii *which is native to the mountains of northern Greece and Albania. There it grows in rock crevices with aubrieta,* Geranium tuberosum *and several small ferns. An architectural little rosette suddenly puts up a hairy stem of flowers maintaining its beauty for weeks.*

Bottom Pulsatilla alpina, *a close relation of our rare native pasque flower, grows on mountain ledges throughout southern Europe. While in flower it is only 10cm (4in) in height, the stem doubles that as it develops its feathery seed head.*

Planting the Rock Garden

If, however, it is the marvellous range of suitable plants that is the reason for wanting a rock garden, then the answers will be different from those already outlined. The rocks will now be less important. They may set the scene or provide desirable niches for certain plants to nestle into but they do not need to be the dominant feature.

The simplest method for rock gardening is merely to use a narrow border, such as that separating the front lawn from the drive, or an isolated area as a 'rock bed'. Little has to be done to make it acceptable to many choice plants. But first some knowledge of the plants' requirements is necessary.

The plants grown in rock gardens are, of necessity, small and are apt to be lumped together under the general title of 'alpines'. This, unfortunately, is a misleading error. Many are from mountainous regions like the mat forming aubrieta and androsace, and the rosettes of the saxifrages and ramondas. But a large number of dwarf rock garden plants are from hot, dry, southern hillsides where their dwarfness is obviously due to different conditions. These include small bulbs such as tulips, hoop-petticoat daffodils and low aromatic shrubs.

The reason why many of these plants from very different habitats will do well together is that both Mediterranean plants and high mountain plants enjoy maximum sun and light; but the latter do not tolerate drought conditions as well as the others. Nonetheless good soil drainage is essential.

The spot chosen should get as much sun as possible. If the soil is at all heavy it will be necessary to improve the drainage. This is done by digging out an area one foot deep and mixing in a layer of stones, broken bricks or gravel into the subsoil. The top soil is then improved by adding moss peat and grit before returning it to the bed.

Above *A small rock bed, however, is more usual as here where the emphasis is less upon the stone than the plants. Here are sempervivums (houseleeks), campanulas, saxifrages and several other typical rock garden plants nestling together against and amongst the rocks to make up almost complete ground cover. The few gaps that are seen have gravel or chippings from which dwarf early spring bulbs – narcissus, tulip, scilla and so on will emerge to ensure the floral interest throughout the seasons. A well-planted rock bed will have flower on virtually every day of the year.*

Left *It is seldom that artificial outcrops can now be made on this scale but if stone is locally available and hence to be had for the cost of cartage it is easier (though more physically exhausting) to think and plan on a large scale. Planting then takes on a similar scale and really fits in with the surroundings.*

Inevitably this treatment raises the bed and this in turn makes sure that winter rains do not hang about to damage the plants. It also produces something of a bank into which a small number of rocks can be laid to set the scene.

The real effect is produced by the growth of the plants which will cover the area in about two years. This is why, with a good choice of plants, a rock bed can give so much pleasure once it has been established, needing little further work or monetary outlay despite the initial effort.

Arrangement of plants should be on the same basis as in the main garden. Points of emphasis are made with dwarf conifers to give all-the-year-round effect. These are sports of junipers, pines and other forest conifers which remain small, taking decades to reach a height of 1.5 to 2m (5 to 6ft). Never plant quick-growing conifers for immediate effect, they will ruin everything. Dwarf shrubs such as certain cotoneasters or brooms can spread over walls or rock faces and dwarf bulbs can push up through the mats of colourful ground cover plants.

Do not be in a hurry for an overnight effect, or the most rampant aubrieta and alyssum will swamp the more delicate subjects.

Rock Plants in Containers

One of the great attractions of rock-garden plants is their gem-like quality; often large flowers borne on disproportionately small growth. Full enjoyment is a hands-and-knees job, especially if they are scented. This is why many specialists prefer to grow their plants in pots in cold frames and bring them into an unheated 'alpine house' for the flowering period. A good alternative is to raise the rock bed by about 60cm (2ft). Maintenance is made easier, further plants can grow in spaces left in the supporting walls and the whole concept is brought nearer to the eyes and nose. A raised bed of this type can happily surround a sitting out area or an edge of a patio.

In the more formal setting of a terrace it is desirable that construction of such a raised bed should repeat something of this feeling. If possible, and especially if one end abuts an existing wall, the material used should be the same as the adjoining building. This does help to give a feeling of continuity by linking the house with the garden.

Often in such a position the raised bed is nothing more than a double wall filled with soil. This seems to be a sadly wasted opportunity as such a position is perfect for so many lovely plants. Why be so mean about it? A width of 1 m (3 ft) would seem a sensible minimum for all but the smallest plots. However, many people would prefer to use such a position for the bigger, brighter flowers provided by seasonal bedding. Remember though, that wallflowers and tulips planted in November have got five months (almost half a year) of absolute dullness before they do anything. And maddeningly they are still in flower when you pull them out to make room for the summer plants. Better, perhaps, is to concentrate seasonal flowers in a number of containers and move them about for the best effect as they come into their own.

Tufa Gardens Often a small garden really has no space for a rock garden or any usual alternative, yet still these little rock plants are coveted. Two possibilities emerge. One is to grow the dwarfest plants in a miniature rock landscape made in a sink. The other is to make literally a rock garden; that is a garden in a single piece of rock.

The second idea is one that is catching on fast, though there must be a limit to the amount of rock available. The type of rock used is tufa, a relatively light-weight porous form of limestone which can hold sufficient moisture for plant growth without permitting lush growth.

A block of tufa weighing about 50 kg (1 cwt) will measure an irregular 45 cm by 45 cm by 30 cm (18 in by 18 in by 12 in). Holes are chipped out (an electric drill with a masonry bit is ideal for the job) in a downwards sloping direction, an

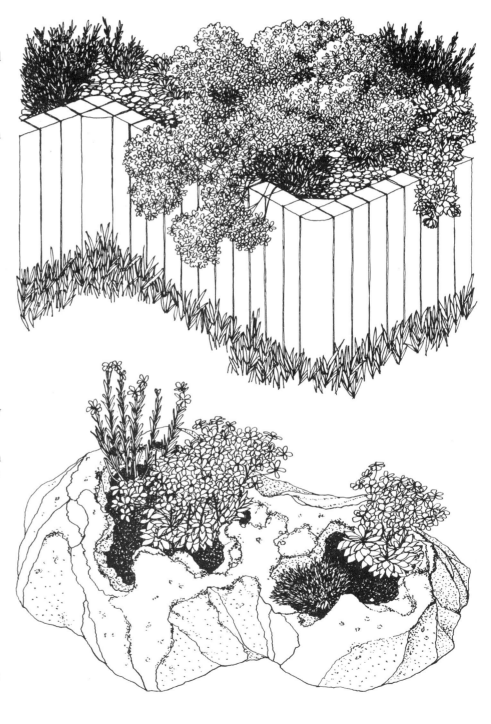

Sites for alpine plants are not restricted to the conventional rock garden. So long as it is remembered what most rock garden plants like, that is good drainage and frequently full sun though with adequate moisture in their growing season, several alternatives are possible. Here are three.

Left Raised beds can be supported by preserved wood stakes. The contained soil can be made to be of any type and so this is one area where calcifuge plants can be successfully grown in a limy area. Drainage is obviously good and irrigation may well be necessary. The size of the bed will determine the scale of plants to be used.

Bottom left On a much smaller scale are single stone rock gardens made of tufa (a light-weight porous limestone which can be easily cut but weathers hard). Holes are drilled and small cushion-forming alpines planted in a little compost.

Below Sink gardens make a balance between the two. They are usually big enough and deep enough to support a sufficient range of plant growth to really make a miniature landscape with dwarf trees both evergreen and deciduous, tiny shrubs and alpine herbaceous plants. Dwarf bulbs can be added to give seasonal colour.

inch or two wide and twice that in depth. Really young alpines, brought from a specialist nursery, are then planted carefully in a compost made up of half coarse sand and half leafmould with some tufa chippings added.

The block should be protected from drying winds if possible, and stand on soil so that it can absorb moisture. Rain is seldom sufficient and indeed watering from above will be necessary initially. If the tufa garden is to be in a courtyard it should stand on a tray of sand which must be kept moist. Tufa gardens are a relatively easy way of growing high alpine cushion or rosette plants that most people find impossible in normal conditions.

Sink Gardens These are less specialist but because of their small size, similar individual attention is possible. Few people can now find (or afford) the lovely old natural-stone sinks that used to be a feature of farmyards. But the deep glazed sinks – so often thrown away when a house is being modernised – can be nearly as good. The depth is right and the shiny white glaze can be perfectly disguised by making a mixture of 2 parts coarse sand to 1 part of peat to 1 part cement (by volume) with water. Then apply this to the outside of the sink.

The end result is a container of perhaps 1 sqm (3 sqft) which can hold an upright conifer such as *Juniperus communis compressa* or a tiny pencil-like cypress is ideal, a small spreading shrublet or two, some dwarf bulbs and a few rosette plants. It can provide interest throughout the year. One immediate advantage is that ideal soil can be given to plants such as autumn gentians, otherwise impossible to grow when the garden soil is limy.

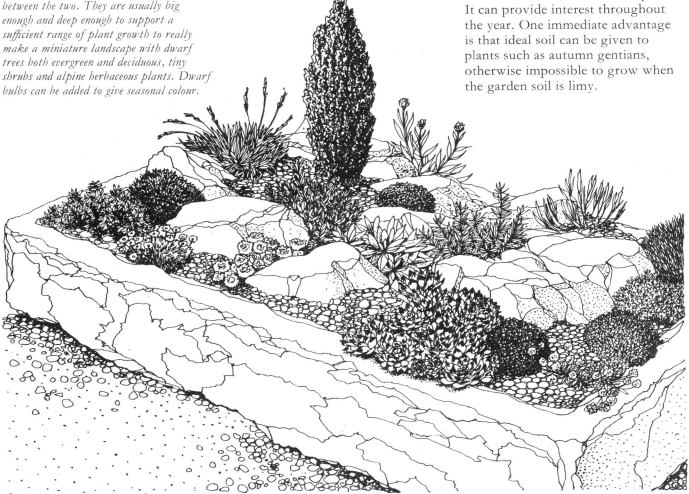

Lawns and Ground Cover

NO HORTICULTURAL PLEASURE IS greater than to see a splendid British lawn again, having been abroad on however exotic a holiday. This is something that we can do really well. So much indeed is a lawn considered to be an inevitable ingredient of the garden scene, that lawns are attempted in areas that are either patently unsuitable or completely unnecessary. People even have lawns when mowing the grass is for them an exact preliminary to purgatory.

It is wise therefore to ask several questions. What is a lawn for? Do we want one? Why? How is it to be used? How much effort am I willing to expend upon it? And so on. In so many cases the lawn (or 'bit of

Ground cover does not have to be of a single monocultural species.

Below A juxtaposition of colourful and leafy plants which leave no room for weeds.

Right A perfect lawn; the epitome of Marvell's often quoted phrase 'A green thought in a green shade'.

grass' as it might be more honestly called) is just that area of space which is not wanted for actual cultivation. Unfortunately to turn the bit of grass into a lawn is possibly an even more laboursome occupation.

These remarks, however, are not made to 'knock' lawns; on the contrary they are chosen to encourage good lawns in the right places. In our climate few large garden scenes without grass look even remotely satisfactory. Lawns are, after all, that part of a garden which link our plot most obviously with the 'natural' world of the English countryside. The reason why the great landscapers of the 18th century were able to incorporate the utter foreignness of Palladian buildings into the shires was their insistence upon a lack of visual division between garden and park. Both were countryside or, conversely, the country was seen for the first time as wholly garden. And that garden was, basically trees set in grass.

Lawns in Small Gardens

On a smaller scale our flower and shrub borders rising from grass present in essence a similar picture. Other plants both set off and are set off by the grass. The smaller the scale, however, the more impeccable the grass needs to be; the more perfect the lawn. This is something of a paradox, because lawn is also access to the borders: the smaller its extent the bigger the wear upon it and the more difficult to maintain visual perfection. This is the point at which the question 'to grass or not to grass?' becomes vital.

Small front gardens, so often seen as a patch of tired grass with a 60cm (2ft) border on all sides must give the negative answer. So too a shady town garden with high walls and trees. It is so often forgotten that 'lawn' is not a plant species but a plant community. It comprises of a number of species of grasses

Hypericum calycinum

Polygonum affine

chosen for their ability to withstand constant cutting which mat together to form a tight sward. All plant communities (especially contrived ones) are continually being attacked by other plant species trying to find a place in the sun for themselves. If they succeed they become part of that community at the expense of one or several of the original members. The direct analogy with lawns and lawn weeds is clear.

With such basic biological pressures accepted it becomes easier to answer the questions posed. If a lawn is required in a small garden it must not receive much wear so through traffic must be catered for. Grass paths less than 2m (6ft) wide are likely to turn to mud at some stage during the year; further wear compounds the problem. Lawn expected to take children's games cannot be a perfect sward. No matter – a garden is for use – but the seed mixture must be chosen with this in mind. In larger gardens or a cottage garden situation only some of the grass needs to be 'lawn'. Rather as the great 18th-century gardens divided at the ha-ha it is sensible to divide at the place where the cylinder lawn mower gives way to the twice or thrice a year rotary cut with lawn paths through it. Garden giving way to orchard or trees and shrubs in grass is the idea.

And here comes the opportunity of working with, rather than against, the biological pressures of competition. With infrequent mowing a number of fine plants can be introduced to make such a position of great beauty. Bulbs, from January snowdrops to November colchicums, will succeed. Broad-leaved herbaceous plants such as lupins, ox-eye daisies, aquilegias will happily co-exist. This is returning, in fact, to natural meadow: grass studded with flowers where daisies, buttercups and even a dandelion or two are part of the *mille fiori* scene, not cause for shame.

Ground Cover

A continuation of this process of
acceptance of broad-leaved species
in grass is to reverse the coin and
see the broad-leaved as the basic
ground cover. Grasses then become
the interloping weeds. Lawns of
other-than-grass are attempted but
are seldom a full success – only
grasses have the ability to grow
continually from the base of their
leaves and hence present a green
top. Chamomile, thymes, cotula and
sagina have occasional adherents but
are best considered as interesting
ground-carpeting species rather than
alternative lawn makers.

Accepting this, the range of plants
to use to cover ground to avoid
bare patches (soil in the garden is,
as has been said, a medium for
growing beautiful or useful plants
in, not an aesthetic experience in its
own right), to reduce weeding, to
furnish ground level texture is
enormous. Several excellent books
on this subject alone are available.
Suffice it to say here that admirable
species can be chosen for all sites
and conditions to help to 'fully
furnish' the garden scene.

Ground cover plants fulfil one
very particular and necessary role:
they bring that desirable cohesion
which links isolated beds, shrubs
and trees. These then grow up from
complementary textures and colours
rather than from bare earth. It
should not be believed that ground
cover species are entirely labour-free:
they are not though they are labour-
saving. But the difference in effect
when this method is used, instead of
the dead hand of herbicides to avoid
weeding, is enormous.

There are two particular considerations to take into account. Is the
ground cover the dominant plant or
community of plants or is it to be
the lowest level in an artificial
reproduction of natural plant
stratification. Both roles are
important but clearly the plant
species chosen will be very different
to cope with the full exposure likely

Waldsteinia ternata

Santolina

Thyme

Phlox subulata

to occur in the former case.

Good lawns demand good
treatment and where this is difficult
to supply the alternative ground
cover role comes in. Banks on
falling sites or those made when
cutting in a driveway are frequent
examples. Solid planting here both
holds the soil and reduces
maintenance. The scale of the area
to be covered, the type of soil,
climate and aspect will all – as with
any other planting problem –
combine to determine the plants
chosen. If the site is not too large a
single species can be very effective:
Hypericum calycinum the lovely Rose
of Sharon, is fine in full sun or half
shade but as it ramps about it is best
isolated by grass above and below;
any suckers appearing there are just
mowed out. Many of the low
Mediterranean shrubs, lavenders and
santolinas and so on are suitable,
too, for hot dry banks. In shade,
ivies are an excellent choice with
variegated forms being particularly
attractive.

On a larger scale cascading plants
such as *Rosa × paulii* and 'Max
Graf', *Cotoneaster microphylla* or
C. salicifolia 'Repens' and evergreen
juniper *Juniperus communis* 'Depressa
Aurea' and *J.c.* 'Wiltonii' are but
some of the numerous possibilities.

Ground cover must also be
considered for normal ornamental
areas. This is the stratification role.
Trees will have shrubs underneath,
shrubs herbaceous plants, and bulbs
and ferns inhabit the lowest level.
In the wild, whole quantities of
species, often very beautiful plants,
have become specially adapted to
succeed in such situations. These
are the plants to look for. Even
under roses, which are traditionally
kept in isolation, small ground cover
plants, pansies and violas, muscari
and polyanthus can add to the
garden scene offering flower when
the roses themselves are still bare
and foliage to mute their summer
colour. Only one word of warning
is necessary. Some very valuable

Geranium cinereum

Erica carnea

ground cover plants, which are ideal for large sites, are dangerously invasive in small gardens if not kept under control. *Lamiastrum galeobdolon* and the bigger periwinkles are examples of these. Treat them with care; if not rigorously thinned out twice a year they will clamber into the lower branches of large shrubs, while the positions of smaller ones are noted by smooth mounds of the ground cover, not unattractive but not intentional either.

If a large area is to be planted with any of the naturally self-layering species – and most indeed have this ability and is why they do their job so well – it is worthwhile to plan at least a year in advance by buying a relatively small number of stock plants, lining them out in a convenient unused spot and encouraging layers by pegging down the horizontal shoots as they appear. In this way a considerable number of plants are cheaply raised and, just as important, they are on the spot to be moved to their permanent site when they are needed. Such forethought can save a lot of money as well as being immensely satisfying.

Ground cover here really means full garden furnishing with the space being used to its maximum to support herbaceous plants, shrubs, climbers and trees in a range of shapes, textures and forms to build up the garden picture we see. Seasonally different plants emerge and flower then go to rest and in this way ground cover as an individual technique is quite unnecessary. This is just good gardening, pure but not really very simple. However it is a technique readily learned as more and more plants are recognised and cultivated.

Containers

SINKS HAVE ALREADY BEEN
discussed as a way of containing a
very specialist type of garden in a
very small space. 'Containerised'
plants of other types have many
advantages too. They can be moved
around to give different effects;
things looking their best come to
the front while those that have gone
over can be put out of sight entirely.
Both permanent and seasonal plants
can be used. A well-chosen shrub,
though necessarily of smallish size,
which may be fine enough in the
open garden gains an added
dimension when growing in a
suitable container. It becomes placed
on a pedestal; branches which
normally brush the soil or get
mixed up with lower-growing plants
hang elegantly over the edge.

A favourite tub of mine for ten
years before the wood disintegrated
held one plant of *Pieris forrestii* and
another of a dwarf, white azalea,
Rhododendron mucronatum. For weeks in
spring it was a most arresting sight;
first brilliant scarlet new growth and
flowers of the pieris, and then as
these were fading the azalea took
over. Then, in early summer I
always planted a couple of morning
glories (ipomoea) to clamber in the
branches and hang out those
incredible blue, trumpet-like blooms.
Even when these were done the two
original shrubs were tidily evergreen
throughout the winter. And all this
in a 60cm (2ft) high tub made of
marine plywood. Such an example
shows at once a further advantage
of container gardening: a difficult
soil is no longer a bar to growing
anything. Here lime-haters flourished
in a chalky area in prepared
compost.

*There is no lack of good containers for
garden decoration. Classical shapes in
modern materials; reconstituted stone and
fibre glass (for few of us can afford the real
thing) are still among the best so long as
there is sufficient depth for good root growth.
Here is a random selection.*

Urns, Pots and Planters

The range of containers available is
enormous; from antique urns in
stone and lead to simple flower pots.
Few people have pockets deep
enough for the former but very
acceptable reproductions of
traditional shapes are made in
reconstituted stone or glass fibre. It
is necessary, however, to be sure
that the interior is large enough to
hold sufficient soil to allow plants to
flourish. Without this the container
has to become an ornament in its
own right and its visual quality
must be really good as it must do
without plant growth to help it
along.

Frequently the modern simple
shapes of asbestos or concrete
(often known as planters) are more
in keeping with a contemporary
patio. Again, soil depth is apt to be
insufficient. Those great saucers

look well enough but it is not easy
to keep plants growing happily in
them. On a larger scale are circular
concrete sewer pipe sections, these
are almost raised beds in themselves.
They lose the virtue of mobility
but can look splendidly architectural
set into cobbles or granite sets. The
sides, of course, can be 'Snow-
cemmed' to tone with adjacent
buildings or walls.

Containers do not have to be so
specialised. It is easy to make them
using rot-resistant marine plywood.
Half barrels are frequently used and
old-fashioned breadcrocks are still
sometimes available. In all cases
drainage must be perfect. If it is not,

holes will have to be drilled so excess water can drain away. Terracotta or earthenware can be drilled with an electric drill; a ring of small holes is made and then the centre, an inch or two in diameter, carefully knocked out.

Growing Medium

Container gardening is a concentrated form of gardening. Obviously, if plants are to remain healthy for years together, a clear feeding regime must be followed. Firstly the soil must be right.

If only a couple of pots are in question it is not too extravagant to buy a prepared compost. John Innes Potting Compost No 3 would be suitable; the texture is open and it releases nutrients over a long period. On a larger scale it is necessary to mix one yourself. The John Innes Potting Compost recipe is

7 parts by volume of sterilised loam
3 parts by volume moss peat
2 parts by volume coarse grit
fertiliser additive – 1 kg per cubic
   metre (2lb per cubic yard)

The same basis applies for a home mix, the peat and grit (*not* builder's sand, it is too fine) are easily bought, loam will have to be the garden soil. However, if this is intractable clay, very thin sand or full of lumps of chalk, then a better source must be found. A mix of six parts of garden soil, three parts of peat and two parts of grit is probably right, plus 1 kg (2lb) of John Innes Fertiliser base to each cubic metre (cubic yard) of soil.

What to Plant

A container holding a single shrub to give year-round effect can usually be helped by the addition of a few bulbs planted in October to give spring interest and when these are over they can be removed and a few summer annuals put in their place.

The choice of the main plant is important, after all it is in view for much or all of the year. The ideal

shrub would offer a good general appearance, exciting, scented flowers and edible, ornamental fruit. This paragon does exist in the shape of citrus trees – though they are not for chilly northern European gardens. It does explain, however, the virtual obsession for oranges and orangeries in times past. Still, even today, a single fruiting bush can be produced, if heated greenhouse space is available, which can be stood out of doors in the summer.

However, if all the desiderata cannot be had in one plant it becomes necessary to lower one's sights a little. Length of interest is a prime consideration, combined with the ability to accept confined conditions and occasional, accidental neglect. This last fact is why camellias (otherwise ideal with their fine foliage and exquisite flowers) are seldom successful: one dry

Choice of plant follows choice of container and the principles of flower arrangement indoors should be borne in mind. Though, of course, growing plants are not as flexible as cut material. Combinations of colourful annuals with trailing foliage – Paul Crampel pelargoniums with Senecio cineraria for example – are good for summer while hebes and ivies might take over for winter.

period in late summer is all that is needed for all next year's flower buds to fall.

General shape and leaf effect is important to complement the architectural setting in which most containers are arranged. In a shady spot *Fatsia japonica* or a Japanese maple have distinctive foliage; while in the sun, yuccas, particularly the variegated forms, and New Zealand flax (phormium) are most striking. Hebes give flower over a long period and their elegant foliage is held throughout the year except in the harshest weather.

Flowers for Summer

For most people tubs and pots in the garden indicate riots of summer flowers. And what a choice there is. Again it is best to choose those types that develop a good shape, for example petunias make a great deal of growth which cascades down the side of the pot, doubling its size and effectiveness. Avoid tight little upright plants like French marigolds which will stand at attention like so many Lilliputian soldiers in orange hats.

If the container is big enough, a mixture of foliage and flowering plants can be used. A central *Senecio cineraria* surrounded by geraniums, or a mound of fuchsias mixed in with *Helichrysum lanatum*. Remember that in most areas early June is soon enough to put these tender plants outside, although shops and garden centres have them on sale from Easter to trap the unwary. However, if even an unheated conservatory is available the summer show can be bought, potted separately, and got moving before being planted out. On a smaller scale the bathroom or kitchen window sills can be commandeered for May.

Generous planting is the rule, those near the edge should lean outwards to encourage the cascading effect and give more room at the top. Putting half the garden down to summer bedding is now extremely expensive, as well as being out of tune with modern trends. So concentrate these plants in a few containers grouped together, rather than strewn about. This will look more effective, be less time consuming and not so costly.

Plants That Stand the Cold

What to do when the autumn frosts kill the tender sub-tropicals? People with some conservatory space or even a space in the spare bedroom should take cuttings of all but the true annuals in September and pot up a few geraniums. This will leave the containers empty. However a normal spring-bedding programme can be followed with November-planted tulips, daffodils or even hyacinths mixed with wallflowers and similar plants. But they are apt to look forlorn in a prominent position, such as beside the front door. A couple of containers could be used in this way and put somewhere sheltered until they are at their best in April. If a few pots of ivy are kept sunk in a corner of the garden throughout Summer, these can come into their own each November to fill the important front-of-the-house containers.

Window Boxes

All these remarks apply also to window boxes which are, in fact, elongated containers with a rather specific job. Here it is even more important to choose cascading plants; the effect is delightful from the outside and from inside the window the view is not just of a forest of stalks. In the garden it is natural to choose container plants to suit the area concerned. With window boxes the frame of the building and the room indoors must be considered. Avoid, for instance, scarlet geraniums against a red-brick house; choose scented flowers if the window is opened on sunny days or even more specifically plant herbs in the kitchen window box.

Care of Container plants

This is even more important than those in the open garden as their reserves of food and especially water are bound to be low. Permanent plants will require fortnightly liquid feeds from April to September. If any plant looks particularly unhealthy after the winter apply a foliar feed. Plants in window boxes and pots of annuals will enjoy a weekly feed during the summer. Water, of course, must be adequate; and this means daily in hot spells when pots are full of root.

All this indicates that care must be taken with the amount of plants in a container and the siting of them. Avoid window boxes that are difficult to water or tubs positioned far from a tap. Consider how the plants will fare if you are always away for a long summer holiday. However, if well used the concentration of colour or architectural effect from this type of gardening is well worth the trouble.

Two further possibilities with containers:

Left   A classical urn with summer seasonals helichrysum and ivy-leaved pelargoniums.

Below   A wooden tub carries Pieris forrestii *with its scarlet shoots and white lily-of-the-valley flowers and a small white deciduous azalea. Welsh poppies seed themselves about the ground and in the tub. When this spring show is over, a couple of morning glories are put in to clamber about and hang out their exquisite blue trumpets through the summer.*

Front Gardens

THE FIRST IMPRESSIONS OF A HOUSE
and its inhabitants is inevitably given
by the front garden. Even if there is
no such thing, the tub by the door
and the window boxes start to
provide value-judgments in the
visitor or casual passers-by. So to a
sensitive soul, care in the design is
desirable. More important, no doubt,
is the effect the front of the house
has on its owner; does it welcome
or does it sullenly sneer? There are
then two facets here, not easily
reconcilable. If the view in from
outside is of importance; more so is
the view outwards from the
windows into the front garden and
beyond. It is a bit like the dilemma
of choosing to live in an ugly house
looking on to elegant ones or the
other way round. Not an easy
decision to make.

A Setting for the House
The front garden, then, exists to set
off the house (and nothing does this
better than good plants carefully
grouped), to give privacy, to
provide protection from noise, and
in the country, rather basically to
demarcate possession. This last
point is a doubtful attribute
especially in 'open plan' estates.

The use of the front garden for
simple display is a common one,
often because it is not very large.
Here the inward or outward views
are of near equal importance, yet it
would still seem that the main
planting should face the house from
the boundary where that line is far
enough away to make it possible.
Many houses, however, front almost
directly on to the street, both in
cities and in country villages. Here
a narrow border of only half a metre

Left *The ultimate in simplicity – a pair of bay trees clipped like poodles. Sweet bay is a Mediterranean plant so not one to use in the coldest positions especially in tubs when the whole root-ball may freeze.*

Above *Also simple, on a much larger scale is a single specimen tree or shrub – here is* Magnolia soulangeana *in grass. Although such a plant is at its best for three or four weeks of the year, the effect is so dramatic that it is remembered from one year and eagerly anticipated.*

(20in) width under the windows or a couple of flagstones lifted, can provide a remarkable amount of planting space. Plants spill out and soften the hard lines of bricks and mortar rising sheer from concrete or tarmacadam. Strong architectural evergreen plants are vital to provide the furnishing throughout the year. New Zealand flax, yuccas, *Mahonia japonica* and *M.* 'Charity', *Viburnum davidii* or *Juniperus pfitzeriana* are the sort of things needed. There are suitable plants for every aspect. Bright colour is best provided by a tub of bulbs and polyanthus for spring and favourite summer-bedding plants to follow on until October.

Where there is something of a garden, proper uses other than that of merely setting off the house and providing a welcome can be entertained. Much depends on the business of the road which the house fronts on to. A gentle country lane with little traffic can be virtually disregarded, leaving views open to fields beyond. Here design need not vary greatly from that of the garden behind the house. There does not have to be a front and back garden mentality. Aspect is far more important: if the house faces south, this is where the main sitting-out area may need to be; occasional passers-by merely add interest to the scene. However, less secluded houses looking on to a village street or small estate can still use front garden space as extensions to the living area; the design of paving leading to grass and plant borders will make this possible.

In many modern housing estates there is often either a restrictive covenant or a generally accepted agreement that fencing is not erected nor that much is done in the way of digging out flower beds. When some rugged individualist does branch out into a few roses or a bit of summer bedding, the effect is usually lamentable. Such areas offer two useful positions; firstly a border directly against the house edged with paving for the sort of sturdy plants recommended for houses right on the road. They can spill onto the row of slabs and give the house the feeling of really belonging to its site. This is where originality can be shown. Secondly, the grass area then can provide a position for a single plant of note, a broad shrub such as *Magnolia soulangeana* or a single flowering cherry or laburnum would do, even a semi-prostrate juniper could look affective. A multi-stemmed bush often looks much better than a standard tree. Whenever a *real* tree can be planted with space to attain its full size this should be done: nothing is so conducive of giving 'atmosphere' as maturing trees.

Privacy and Protection

Real privacy can, of course, be provided by walls, fences or hedges. Consider first the need for this: if there is quiet and seclusion behind the house its desirable quality will be emphasized by being able to see the world from the front. Older people in particular who do not get out much, often enjoy seeing the world pass by; and in a caring community any help needed can be more easily given.

However if protection is needed, for whatever reason, its type and material must be related to the site. The smaller the area the more formal the surroundings need to be so that a courtyard situation is obtained and the area must be treated as such. It then has its own potential. Large areas can use informal plantings or belts of shrubs and trees and here, ideally, the planting should not merely protect the house and hide the road but conceal the very boundary itself. This gives the impression that the garden goes much further than it actually does; this is a major artifice of effective design.

Access

It cannot be forgotten that a front garden has a job to do – that of access. This is naturally vital and the garden has to be designed around it, without the drive or paths being too visually dominant. Again plant material needs to be strong and permanent to compete with much inanimate concrete and stone. On busy roads it will be necessary to provide extra car parking or even turning space, and hence most of the available area is given over to it. Variation in the materials used will help to avoid the feeling of living in a municiple car park. Where possible, cars should be able to reach the front door, remembering that space concerned is not merely a car's width (visitors are always apt to have quite unnecessarily large machines!) but room for doors to open and allow passengers to get out. Roses and other prickly plants must be avoided. Again, planting and the surface materials must make it perfectly clear where cars and people may go and indeed are required to go. The 'tradesman's entrance' as a label on a door or gate is almost a thing of the past, but good design must make it quite clear who can go where.

Two further ideas in front gardens:

Right Here, right onto the street, a simple 18th Century house has a garden of little more than a metre in depth. Where the house front itself is agreeable it is a mistake to hide it behind curtains of creepers. Better to concentrate on interesting planting at ground level of all the year round interest. Here are Phormium tenax variegatum, Mahonia japonica, purple Japanese maples and cistus. Other things seed into the paving cracks and enjoy the sunny situation.

Below A cottage garden comprises of an exercise in ground cover. A happy miscellany of columbines, Welsh poppies, irises and pansies tumbling about so as almost to obscure the front door.

Garden Buildings

Much correspondence in the gardening weeklies seems to be devoted to methods of hiding ugly garden sheds. No doubt if an inherited structure is a monstrosity something must be done, but when gardens are being planned from scratch the problem is very different. Integration into the chosen scheme becomes visually desirable and ergonomically essential. Garden sheds are for use, so access must be easy and unencumbered by plant growth. As with greenhouses initial choice of design is vital; even within a given price range the acceptable and the dreadful invariably rub shoulders.

Two very different ideas of a garden shelter :

Left *This garden house, with its trellised back and near ogee-shaped roof, has a strong feeling of the Brighton Pavilion ('As if', said Sidney Smith, 'St. Paul's had gone to the sea and pupped.')*

Below *In complete contrast is this American-inspired A-shaped design with its slatted frames.*

Summer Houses

In small gardens the idea of a garden house or summerhouse may seem superfluous. Yet a small structure designed as a focal point to provide little more than a covered seat, may provide sufficient of the conventional tool shed needs without devolving into the fully utilitarian. It can still house a couple of folding chairs and a few well-oiled tools (not an unpleasing sight in themselves) can hang on the back wall.

Such a conception fits admirably into the scheme when the back of the house faces north. Here the conventional sitting-out area immediately outside is predominantly in shade, so this essential part of a garden for living in has to move down into the sun. In such

situations the view back to the house becomes so much more important. Obtaining privacy in a terrace garden is more difficult.

Screening

The view back is apt to take in those inevitable but unaesthetic features such as an oil-tank or coal bunker, or both. Again access for both delivery and visits from the house, in the case of solid fuel these are at least daily, must be arranged for ease and convenience. The coal man is unlikely to have time to take great care of a cherished screen with a hundredweight sack on his back. It is a help if they can be linked directly with any stepping of a wall as in the case of a protruding chimney breast. The screening wall or fence can then more satisfactorily follow an already existing line. Care is necessary to minimise the effect of any such screen, or it only serves to draw attention to that which is supposed to be out of sight.

Right   A rather grandiose garden house of treated pine. It is raised on a plinth of paving and is entered by sliding doors. Such a building needs siting to obtain maximum sun. Protection from wind is obtained from a backing on the north of tall trees.

Below   Much simpler is this open framed shelter. The canopy, when clothed with climbers, gives restful summer shade.

Greenhouses

Why do i want a greenhouse? The answers may appear obvious, but it is wise to ask this question. Is the requirement a sun-trap extension to the house with ornamental plants as part of the general ambience and decor? Is it to provide a controlled environment in which to cultivate a specialist range of species? Is it to propagate and grow on a range of plants for the kitchen garden and for the summer-bedding schemes? Or is it, as is so often attempted, all three and growing room for a few tomato plants besides?

Choosing a Greenhouse
Much the wisest, because it determines the type of greenhouse chosen, is to make the decision as to the expected prime use. But accept in advance that if this is all the glasshouse space available, other things will creep in however strongly the initial feeling was. Of course, the omnipresent spectre of cost comes at an early stage and affects the size, materials and whether the structure is to be custom-built, off-the-peg or do-it-yourself. It becomes highly desirable to discover from advertisements in the gardening press just what is available, and to examine at leisure all the literature you can find.

The conventional lean-to conservatory leading from a room in the house has much to commend it (they were almost *de rigeur* on untold thousands of suburban houses of the 1920's and 1930's). The method has an origin which began rather grandly with Victorian 'winter gardens' full of palms and ferns. In those very different days the conservatory was seen to isolate the house, at least on that side, from the vagaries of a northern climate. Now we see it more as a transition between indoors and outdoors. All three areas have their part to play in agreeable modern living, with movement from one to another being made easy.

Free-standing greenhouses have certain advantages which lean-to's lack. Light is usually better (this is vital to avoid spindly growth) but there are disadvantages. Heat-loss through wind is greater and the smaller the house the proportionally more of a problem this will be. So much so that there is little point trying to heat the smallest houses in winter at all; for each time the door is opened half the greenhouse atmosphere is exchanged at a stroke unless it is approached through

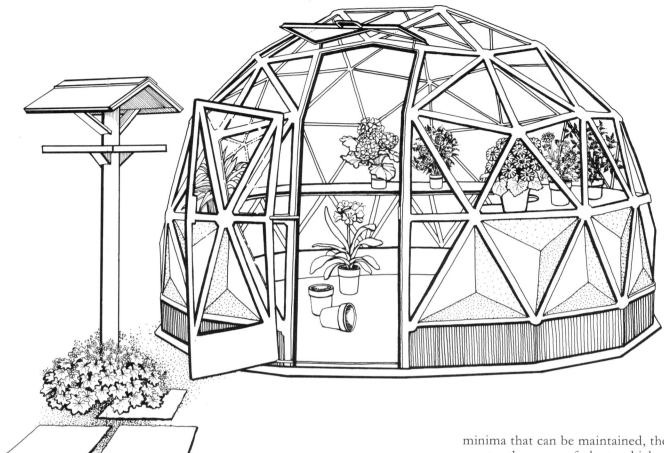

The wish to grow a wider range of plants than is possible in the open garden by providing something of a controlled environment has produced a bewildering range of greenhouses. They come in all sizes, materials and shapes. With a number of different heating methods and varying amounts of automation, prospective buyers should try to decide clearly what they wish to grow and then to buy the biggest greenhouse they can afford.

Left *A conventional lean-to greenhouse.*

Above *A geodesic dome.*

another building, a garden shed or the garage – in which case it ceases to be free standing.

Small isolated greenhouses are also not easily sited satisfactorily in the garden. Manufacturers realising this have attempted to help by producing models in different shapes such as the attractive octagons and geodesic domes. But these do not help the difficulties of successfuly producing a fine range of plants in a single regime. Such shapes, indeed, are even less easily compartmentalised than conventional greenhouses.

Heating

Greenhouse heating is expensive but without a certain amount, to keep the place at least frost-free, cold-weather displays are bound to be at a minimum. The higher the winter

minima that can be maintained, the greater the range of plants which will succeed. Whatever is decided as being economically acceptable it is desirable to arrange a small separate section (perhaps no more than a propagating frame with undersoil heating) to be warmer than the rest of the house and a nearby cold frame. Immediately three regimes become available which make possible a progression of growth stages. This is how municipal greenhouses and botanic gardens can keep things looking so well with their range of back-up glass: the same system on a very small scale is possible at home.

Heating Methods
Paraffin – laboursome and potentially lethal to plants.
Electricity
Gas – free-standing calor gas
Solid-Fuel boiler
Connection to house central heating
Solar Panels

Left *In some cases elegance of design and careful arrangement of plants seems to combine the best features of garden house and greenhouse. Sadly this is apt to be fallacious for it works well only if there is another 'working' greenhouse to produce a changing range of plants. However, where this is possible a return, as here, to the late 19th-Century conservatory is contrived.*

Below *Quite different in style is the octagonal greenhouse, which would be suitable for a small garden.*

Range of Regimes

Cold House Alpines, bulbs in pots, azaleas, dwarf conifers. Cold frame necessary in addition. Late seedling raising. Vine is possible.

Cool House Winter minimum 4·5°C (40°F). Forced bulbs and spring flowering annuals. Cinerarias, primulas, pelegoniums. Early vegetable seedlings. Half hardy annuals for outdoors.

Temperate House Winter minimum 10°C (50°F). A few orchids especially cymbidiums, paphiopedilums. Overwintering exotics for summer containers such as daturas, citrus. Winter-flowering primulas and schizanthus. Raising peppers and aubergines.

Furniture

THE USES TO WHICH AREAS OF THE garden are put are directly proportional to their convenience and attractiveness. Each part for living in, whether it is a convenient corner by the back door or a carefully designed terrace, needs furniture just as much as any room indoors. The choice is hardly less wide but an initial divide occurs between furniture which stays out all or most of the time and that which has to be expressly put out for use.

Even a small garden needs a seat or two, or a bench in the warmest corner, which is always there for immediate use, for example for a morning cup of coffee or to string the beans for lunch. Few people, however, would feel justified in making time to take a chair out for so short a time. Convenience is all. Again, if there is one spot which gets late sun, or midday shade or enjoys a particularly beautiful view, this is where a permanent seat should be.

Often, because of its position, the seat is itself a garden feature, an eye-catcher at the end of a path or in another prominent position. This is a spot to concentrate planting which complements the time of day when the seat is most in use: morning glory and cistuses for forenoon use, night-scented stocks, tobacco plants, evening primroses and *Cestrum parqui* for a late-day post-work place.

Materials of permanent seats must be durable. Cast iron or its modern alternative, aluminium alloy, and stone have complete permanence while the most weather-resistant woods, teak and western red cedar, benefit from being taken under cover in winter – although they do not demand it.

The range of garden furniture is, predictably, wide. Here are a few examples:

Top left A wooden collapsible chair and low round table would double happily in a conservatory or even in the house. In use on the lawn, wide legs prevent gradual sinking in.

Below left Hammocks are fine once you have learnt to get into them elegantly – but first grow your trees.

Top right Less for lounging is a Victorian style fern motif bench in metal and wood. Originals are cast iron, immensely heavy and equally expensive. Painted aluminium alloy makes a good alternative and can be moved around without fear of rupture.

Centre right Here is an interesting group of boxes with hinged lids, to get at the interior storage space, and struts which prop them up to serve as back rests. Cushions are brought out as required.

Below right One of the many small barbecue units now available. There is much to be said for having the cooking area at standing height. Although this type can be easily wheeled under cover, a lid is invaluable. There is nothing nastier than a barbecue left out in overnight rain.

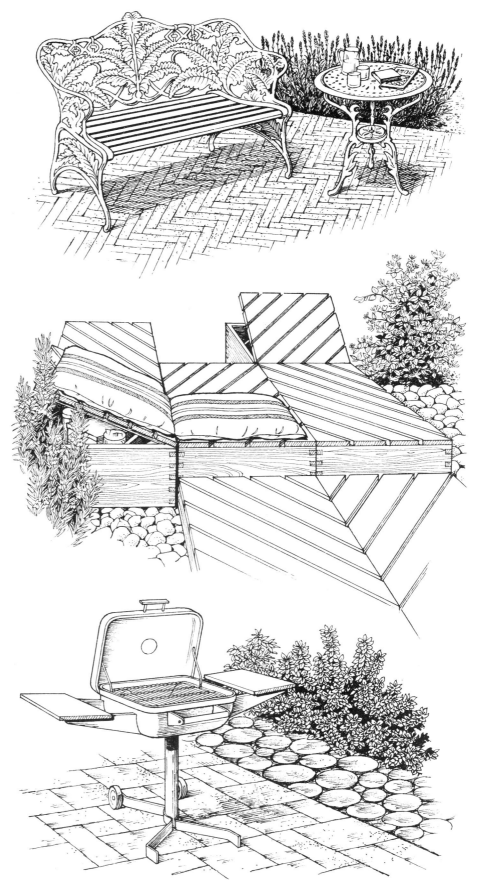

Houses and gardens with a period flavour gain from having furniture to fit that period: reeded iron Regency seats or florid floral Victorian ones add to the feeling. Fortunately any number of good reproductions are now available.

Stone seats naturally weather, though they may take some years to attain that patina we envy when visiting great gardens. Do remember to keep a cushion or two to hand: stone can be very chilly to sit on.

Choice in wooden furniture is wide. Usually the simpler the design the better, and of good solid construction: cheapness seldom equates with economy. Seldom, too, are rustic confections at all satisfactory from the points of view of either comfort or aesthetics.

As a table, a big flagstone, a marble wash-stand top or a piece of slate can all be brought into use with any number of possible permanent supports.

In many cases we need movable garden furniture to take advantage of changing sun and shade. Here the range is even greater and the choice more confusing. In general it should be light to handle and easy to store (where will that great swing-seat go in the winter?). Collapsible designs are frequently the answer but they must be easy to erect. Avoid, too, any type of garden seat or table with thin, spindly legs: the table will tilt alarmingly as it inevitably finds the cracks between paving stones on the terrace and the chairs sink inexorably beneath you into the lawn.

Left *An elegant confection of Regency iron garden furniture (note the feet to the chair legs) under a canopy, all arranged for a civilised meal. Eating outside need not degenerate into a picnic.*

Below *Simpler and in a more modern mode, table and chairs fit equally well into the terrace and raised bed situation for which they have been chosen.*

Lighting and Statuary

MANY OF THE GREAT GARDENS OF the past depended upon inanimate ornaments for much of their effect. In Europe this began as an Italian renaissance idea repeating, as it was thought, the great periods of classical learning and art a thousand years before. Hence statuary representing myths, gods and idealised humans stood about to give point to a vista, to line a terrace and generally to emphasise the fact that a garden was something of a paradise.

As the centre of European culture moved north into France and later into England, the statues, urns, obelisks and pillars continued to be used as focal points in very different situations. They exist in profusion in the daunting formality of 17th-century Vaux-le-Vicomte and Versailles, and with greater restraint at 18th-century Stowe and Stourhead, both epitomes of the English landscape garden. One common factor links these garden ornaments: they were invariably works of art in their own right (it does help here to be the greatest monarch that France ever had or one of England's most prosperous bankers, to be able to pay for such things).

However, those of us who by chance are neither royal nor rich, can still profitably look to success of the past in using the inanimate in the garden scene.

Above *Mass produced concrete statuary presents an awesome sight: a coy boy, a simpering pixy, ducks and a rabbit. Yet, surprisingly, most will find a loving home and some indeed will look well. Even a simple object, well placed and integrated into the scene can add to the interest.*

Right *But a restrained reproduction of a 17th Century sundial is safer and much less likely to pall.*

Choice of Statuary

The objects and the material from which they are made can vary enormously, but a few considerations can help towards their choice and use. Roles are in particular two-fold: to emphasise or give permanent interest to a spot where plants alone cannot quite suffice, and to take the eye and hold it at the end of a viewing-point. 'Vista' may seem too extravagent a word when the eye-catcher (a good 18th-century landscaper's term) is only a few feet away. However, it is valid and as important as the sham castle built on a hill in the next county was in a previous century. Whatever it is, it must add to the garden picture, it must be in scale with its surroundings and must be as good of its type as can be found. A deep pocket is desirable but not essential. Nowadays, to find a piece of old statuary or an elegant urn at an

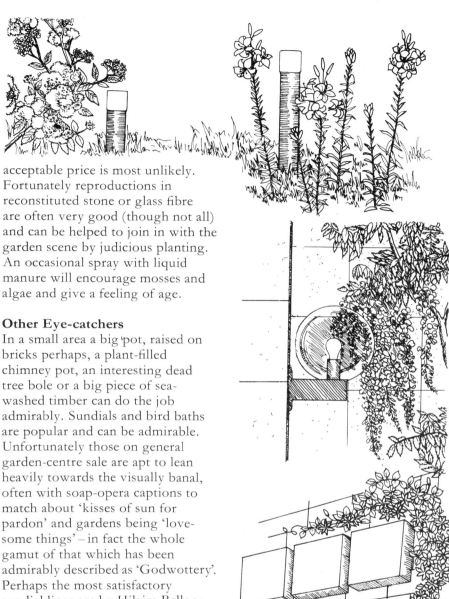

acceptable price is most unlikely. Fortunately reproductions in reconstituted stone or glass fibre are often very good (though not all) and can be helped to join in with the garden scene by judicious planting. An occasional spray with liquid manure will encourage mosses and algae and give a feeling of age.

Other Eye-catchers

In a small area a big pot, raised on bricks perhaps, a plant-filled chimney pot, an interesting dead tree bole or a big piece of sea-washed timber can do the job admirably. Sundials and bird baths are popular and can be admirable. Unfortunately those on general garden-centre sale are apt to lean heavily towards the visually banal, often with soap-opera captions to match about 'kisses of sun for pardon' and gardens being 'lovesome things' – in fact the whole gamut of that which has been admirably described as 'Godwottery'. Perhaps the most satisfactory sundial lines are by Hilaire Belloc:

> 'I am a sundial
> And I make a botch
> Of what is done
> Far better by a watch.'

More important, and apparently obvious, is that a sundial is a nonsense if placed in the shade. Similarly bird baths are no use if positioned in an awkward position for watching the avian visitors.

Snow White, her seven dwarfs and all related gnomes are best left in Disneyland, whence they came. In the garden, coyly placed around the pond where they are quite clearly paying no attention to the equally twee 'No Fishing' notice,

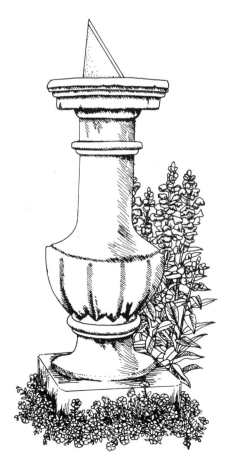

Lighting to illumine an evening meal on the terrace, to make a drive or path safe for residents and visitors or dramatically to floodlight a group of plants seen from the house are just some of its uses. These can take a garden from the ordinary to the definitely different. But the lighting units themselves and the wires that service them should be as inconspicuous as possible.

they may be amusing to begin with but the joke quickly palls.

However, whatever the owner's proclivities in this line – and a garden after all is a place where wishes and likes can be indulged regardless of precious pundits – the fact that some object is obtained and sited indicates its importance in the garden scene. And one area where we gain over grand gardeners of earlier times is our ability to enjoy these things at night by modern lighting techniques. Where a view is part of a lived-in room as well as outdoor garden it is admirable to emphasise it by a spot-light.

Lighting

Similarly if a terrace or other sitting out area is to be used to the full, lighting is well worth considering. Electricity can easily be taken either above or below ground to the requisite spot by a *professional electrician* to avoid danger and ultimately probably save cost.

The range of light holders is now considerable and as with statuary, choice of design is a matter of personal likes or dislikes. Only one thing perhaps should be said: the whole object of the exercise is to enhance the night, in the daytime the holders should be as unnoticeable as possible.

Good statuary is both expensive and difficult to come by.

Left A Portland stone goddess presiding over a riot of foliage.

Right A lead Pan pours water into a tiny tank. Again, with a backdrop of rhododendron and ivy the figure is closely integrated into the garden scene. It becomes a focal point without becoming completely dominant.

Vegetables

Most people with medium-sized gardens have been accustomed to use a part, usually as out of sight as possible, as a kitchen garden. This pattern followed in essence the big country house pattern in which the utility area was separated from the ornamental garden, or pleasure grounds as they were often termed, by high walls and sometimes considerable distances. These old walled, kitchen gardens with trained fruit trees and greenhouses full of exotic crops were masterpieces of gardening skill. However they were not for polite eyes: they were well hidden and only their produce was seen on the dining-room table.

Ideas from Abroad

Such physical and social isolation is no longer the rule even in the grandest of ducal establishments, but its attitude has spread and remains at all levels: flowers round the house, vegetables on the allotment. Certainly this stratification has not been the case on the continent. In France there is the concept of the *potager* in which vegetables and fruit were, and still

Globe artichokes and rhubarb are not difficult to produce and have the added bonus of elegant foliage. Globe artichokes are especially beautiful if the temptation to cut the buds is resisted and the great blue thistle heads allowed to open.

are, used as parts of an ornamental formal plan. This was often of daunting intricacy (that at Villandry on the Loire is a famous example). It probably reflects the esteem in which food and its cooking was held. The potager idea has much to teach us here but, like certain wines, it does not travel well.

Germany too has moved forward in the area of home vegetable gardening. Allotments have been upgraded into 'leisure gardens' (something of a wry joke after a full day of heavy winter digging). The tool shed doubles as a summerhouse – rather like a beach hut – having a small sitting out area enjoying privacy provided by a small tree or hedge. This is a far cry from rusty corrugated iron shacks, crazily leaning amidst last year's dead runner beans. This is the classic, though not necessarily true, expectation of allotment gardening in England. Fortunately such attitudes and prejudices, although dying hard, are on the decline. The boring old homily of necessity mothering invention, does have a certain validity in this context.

The cost of vegetables and fruit in the shops is decidedly erratic and the quality most dubious; flavour frequently giving way to the greater commercial importance of external appearance and the ability to travel well. Exquisite flavour and thin skin are not commercially viable. There is increased interest in food, engendered no doubt, by the frequence of continental travel in the 1960's and dining out in restaurants.

Another movement to encourage home cultivation has been the increase in organically grown food, when the grower knows exactly what has gone into his land. Acceptance that vegetables and fruit need not be aesthetically unacceptable when combined with increased interest and economic necessity, have engendered a revolution in home kitchen gardening. All have been helped by the plant breeders who are year by year bringing out new varieties especially for the home producer.

Varieties of vegetables and fruit once impossible without glasshouses are now available, such as sweet peppers and aubergines; Brussels sprouts are more evenly formed and less 'cabbagy' and melons ripen under cloches. Frequently they are described as F_1 hybrids; these are the products of a carefully controlled cross between two parents, each offering particularly desirable characteristics which combine in the hybrid. They do not, however, breed true a second year and the cross has to be made anew. This is why gardeners are advised not to collect seed from F_1 hybrids.

What to Grow

In planning any area of vegetable garden it is wise to think carefully of what you and your family most enjoy. There is no point in sowing a couple rows of turnips if you cannot bear to eat them, just because the gardening column in the newspaper tells you this is the time to sow. In choosing crops it is also sensible to consider what is usually expensive in the shops and which vegetables loose their freshness quickly. A crisp lettuce straight from the garden in high summer is so different from one that has been sitting on a shelf for a couple of days. Vegetables such as potatoes which store admirably, should only be grown after everything else has been fitted in. This does not apply to earlies which need to have their skins rubbed off and be cooked at once.

Here are three vegetables to show how certain characteristics have been encouraged to suit the tastes of man. Carrot is an example of a swollen root, cauliflower is the development of the flower head and lettuce shows the leaves forming a basal rosette.

Understanding Vegetables

It must be realised that all vegetables are plants which have been selected by man to develop some form of leaf, stem, root or even flower which is good to eat. In his breeding those specific parts have been exaggerated far beyond the original plant. Wild carrot, for example, or parsnips have virtually nothing below ground worth eating. In order to build up a huge food stores (which the plant is unconsciously doing in the hope that it can use them next year to push up flower spikes which will in turn seed to reproduce the species) these crops need careful cultivation and feeding. There is little mystique about this; it is set out in all the tomes dealing with the subject, or better, begin to understand the plants as organisms. Then in many cases common sense helps with garden problems.

It might be expected that leaf vegetables require a different feeding emphasis from the root crops and again from those whose fruits (such as peas and beans) are eaten. It is logical, too, if different groups of plants take up different proportions of nutrients from the soil to make sure that no crop stays on the same area of land year after year. Rotations are not only a subject for agricultural history, they also make sense to today's gardeners. Pest and disease build up will be less, too.

It is wise to distinguish between plants which respond more favourably to certain conditions because of their original habitat. Runner beans and sweet peppers, for instance, are from the tropics and hence need as much sun and warmth as possible (that is why they are so good, if well fed and watered, in town courtyards). Cabbages and their tribe are plants from northern Europe so are not likely to suffer when exposed to British weather. The exception are cauliflower varieties expressly bred for the special growing conditions of Cornwall or Brittany.

Cropping Plan of the Vegetable Garden

Courgettes
Peas
French beans
Tomatoes

Swedes
Celeriac
Carrots
Beetroots
Spring onions
Lettuces
Radishes

Radishes
Lettuce
Shallots
Onions
Leeks
Spinach

Cabbages
Brussels sprouts
Cauliflower
Early Potatoes

In order to carry out a crop rotation programme to avoid a build up of pests and diseases, change the blocks of plants round each year. The edges of herbs and soft fruit will occupy the same space every year as will the wigwam of runner beans in the centre.

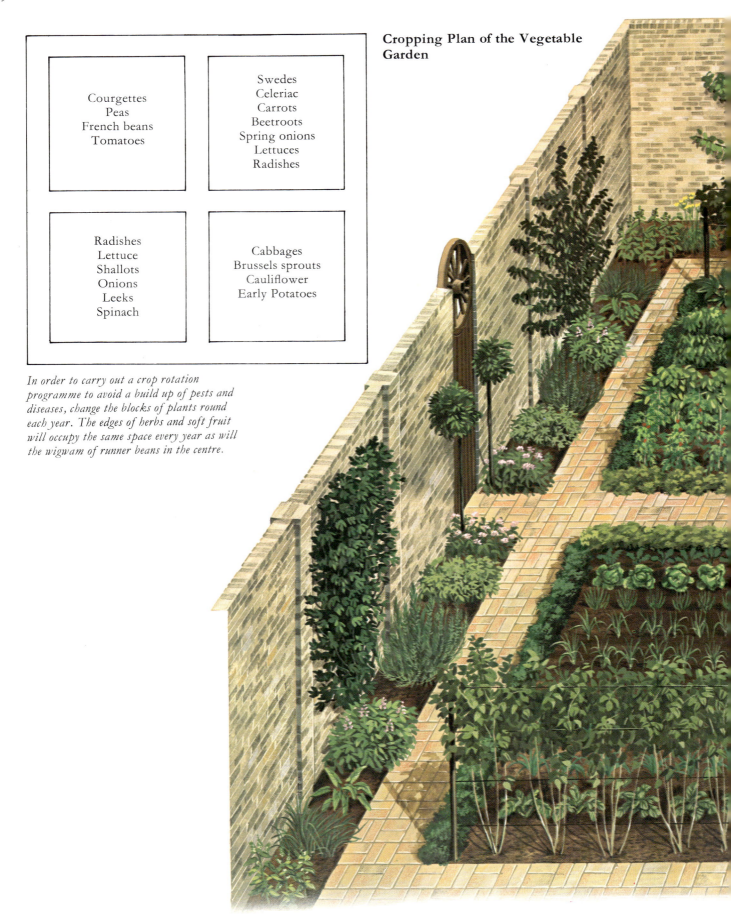

Carrots are originally from dry chalk uplands, parsnips from moist meadows; their ecological background still affects them in the garden. Cultivation, feeding and irrigation obviously ameliorate local conditions but here again these must be worked with: aubergines and melons are not for cold northern gardens, nor asparagus, a plant of sandy shores, for heavy, wet clay.

Crops for Small Gardens

The most suitable crops for small gardens are those coming to quick maturity, so that the ground can be used again for a second or even third crop in the year. The traditional fallow autumn and winter digging all at one time will never happen – short rows, individual cultivation will be the rule. Big perennial crops will not justify a row but in some cases can be used in the ornamental garden. Asparagus grown over 3sqm (3.3 sqyd) will give fortnightly cuttings, enough for two or three people from April to late June. From then on a cloud of delightful feathery foliage results with a clear, yellow autumn colour. Globe artichokes provide some of the most striking grey leaves in all the garden. Rhubarb could be similarly considered for its decorative value. These are not necessarily plants for the big garden if not considered solely in the traditional manner of growing.

It is not very likely that anyone would put their whole back garden down to vegetables and fruit, but if it were done with care and considerable effort it could be visually attractive throughout the year – as well as making the family nearly self-supporting. Alternatively the picture can illustrate an enclosed kitchen garden on the traditional pattern with not an inch of ground or wall space wasted as crop follows crop. They do not, of course, all mature at the same time, in fact an art of this aspect of gardening is to ensure succession.

Fruit

THERE ARE FEW HOME PLEASURES quite so satisfying as picking the first bowl of raspberries of the season or a ripe juicy pear from one's own tree. As with vegetables, both soft and top (or tree) fruit used to be kept well away from the house. Exceptions were in cottage gardens where a delightful miscellany of fruit and flowers were quite customary and today some of the most successful of country gardens, often around renovated old cottages, still enjoy this mix. It has much to commend it.

Even in the smallest courtyard it is possible to use a wall for a plant that will give fruit as well as looking good; after all it has got to flower first. Similarly if a garden has room for only one tree (at the back, it should be said; fruit in the front garden is far too tempting for local lads) might this not be a pear or apple, or in sheltered positions a peach grown as a standard. All these are lovely in the spring (like the conventional flowering cherries) and the autumn crop of fruit is then a bonus. Sweet cherries are also a possibility, but a single tree attracts birds from all around who are not averse to gobbling the fruits just before they are ripe. To see this happening before one's eyes is as frustrating an experience as can be imagined.

Trained Trees
All fruit trees are bought either grafted or budded onto a rootstock. Each tree is a combination of a rootstock which controls the ultimate size and the scion which is growing upon it. This will be the variety such as cooking apple

'Bramley's Seedling' or dessert pear 'Conference' for example. Correctly chosen rootstock make it possible to grow tree fruit in very restricted ways such as cordons, pillars, dwarf pyramids and espaliers. Vigorous stocks are used for standards or half-standards.

As with vegetables in the French potager, fruit trees are used as part of the basic design and are trained into a number of forms. Again, whilst not advocating a slavish anglicisation of the gallic mode, it

Two methods of training fruit trees.

Below Cordon apples crop heavily and can also form an attractive screen in the garden.

Right A mature fan-trained pear would look handsome against any south- or west-facing wall. It too could form a screen if trained against wires.

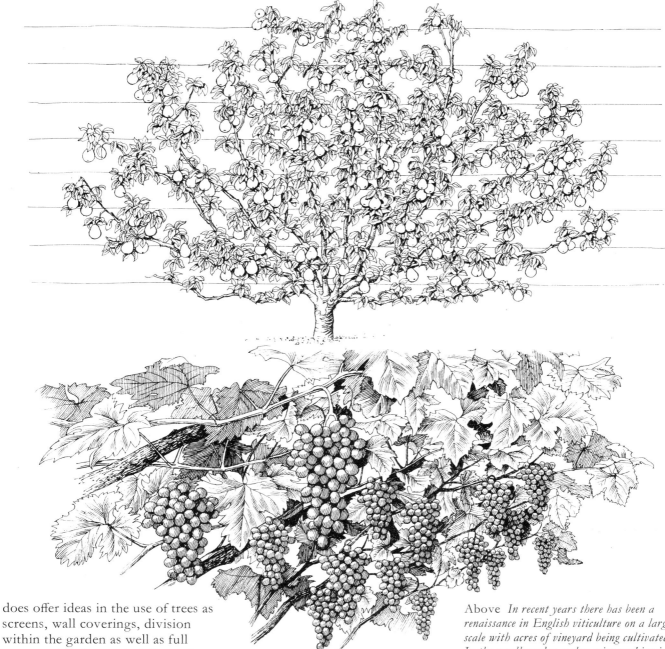

does offer ideas in the use of trees as screens, wall coverings, division within the garden as well as full trees to give the vertical dimension which new gardens in particular lack. Pears and apples take kindly to trained forms; they can be bought with the shape already begun and subsequent pruning is not difficult.

Stone fruit – plums or peaches – are much less easy to deal with. There are no fully satisfactory dwarfing rootstocks for these. Although fan-trained peaches are universally recommended, in all but the coldest areas and those subject to late-spring frosts, an open ground bush form in a lawn or as the tall plant in a small shrub border is perhaps better. It is also less difficult to prune and often producing very good crops. In all normal situations plums have to be grown as full-sized, small trees.

Pollination
Top fruit offer one further problem when grown as single specimens or

Above *In recent years there has been a renaissance in English viticulture on a large scale with acres of vineyard being cultivated. In the small garden, unless wine making is a prime interest, it is perhaps best to use a warm wall for one of the varieties which in a good season will ripen good sized grapes to dessert sweetness. When the weather fails to come to standard it may be still possible to make an acceptable wine from grapes hanging on until October.*

in small quantities and that is that the flowers of many varieties are self-sterile. This means that pollen from another variety which is compatible with the self-sterile tree must be available if fruit is to develop; and that, after all, is the whole point. So if planting is to take place in an area away from other suitable trees, a self-fertile variety must be chosen from the catalogues. It is not enough just to find a good-looking tree in the local garden centre and hope for the best.

Soft Fruit

Soft or bush fruit is generally little trouble: annual pruning of raspberries, blackberries and loganberries is simple, consisting of cutting out all growth that has fruited as soon as the crop is picked.

Blackcurrants are treated similarly and red and white currants and gooseberries are not very difficult. These last three flower and fruit on spurs which develop on mature branches rather in the way of pears. They can, like pears, be trained as cordons or with several stems against a wall forming a fan. A well-fruited redcurrant in such a position can look magnificent and offering a difficult choice – whether to leave them a bit longer to adorn the garden or pick them at once for the table.

Situation

Wall and fences of most aspects offer sites for fruit. Redcurrants and gooseberries, morello cherries and the hardier apples will take the north side. Eastern aspects which catch the early-morning sun are best avoided because spring frosts on the flowers will not have time to thaw gently and the potential crop will be ruined. South and west aspects offer sites for the choicest apples and especially pears. Many of these, such as Williams' Bon Chrétien and Doyenné du Comice, have French names indicating their southern origin.

Exotic Fruit

Even more exotic fruit are possible in warm positions. They may not give a certain crop every year, but taken as a part of the ornamental garden they are frequently of sufficient general interest in themselves, not to make this vital.

Figs have striking foliage; Chinese gooseberries (*Actinidia chinensis* is one of the New Zealand hermaphrodite forms), persimmon and, of course, grapes are possibilities, as are open garden trees – medlars, quince (no fruit smells better) and delicious mulberries. The range of plants is extraordinarily wide and emphasises that the normally few really interesting trees seen are by no means the only things worth planting. A difficulty is to find a source.

It is quite possible to get fine crops of fruit from one or two trees, apple, pear, plum or peach, so long as attention has been paid to pollination, compatibility and time of flowering if there are few other fruit trees in nearby gardens. Such trees are considered more as part of the general garden scene for their size and spring flower; the possibly erratic crop comes as a happy bonus or even, in years of glut, something of an embarrassment. But that is the form of fruit to go for if pruning other than the taking out of an occasional crossing branch is as much as one can be bothered with.

That is a perfectly valid approach and often pays off happily. But if a range of fruit, both in type and season (it is possible, without great specialist knowledge or storage facilities to eat home-grown apples from August to April) is required then a number of varieties will be needed. These are best grown in some trained and restricted fashion. Dwarf pyramid and pillar forms need no support but cordons and espaliers do. Here is shown a fine Ellison's Orange apple about 8 to 10 years old with seven tiers of branches.

Plums and peaches are grown as fan-trained forms because of the need to replace fruiting wood annually. This is definitely a more difficult technique, especially as no reliable dwarfing stock for stone fruit has yet been developed.

The All-Year-Round Garden

THE IDEA THAT ALL GARDEN pleasures have to be tidied away every year with the terrace furniture at the end of September is at last dying a well-deserved death. This school of thought insisted that nothing remained but to get the vegetable garden dug over and then to retire indoors with the seed catalogues and a pile of detective novels until the following spring. Fortunately this is a travesty of the truth. Gardens are, or should be, capable of providing year-round pleasures. Pleasures for the eyes, nose and taste buds in every month of the twelve. They will be different and indeed should be evocative of their season.

A Christmas rose or a winter iris are the treats they are, not only because they are beautiful flowers, but because they flower when they do. Similarly vegetables and fruits *in their season* fresh from the garden are one of the prime pleasures of a gourmet's and a gardener's life. Much more so, I would suggest than strawberries, for example, flown from California in January at incredible expense.

Of course, the first peas or the earliest daffodils in pots are delightful. The pleasures they afford are enhanced by anticipation. But however delicious to the senses, the power of each to charm is bound to be diminished by twelve month availability were it possible. A big enough garden and a deep-freeze to match does make this possible nowadays in almost every way. But the almost is a big one. Even when flavours are hardly distinguishable (perhaps only true of peas) from the really fresh a dullness creeps in from

Mahonia japonica

Elaeagnus pungens '*Maculata*'

repetition and the lack of looking forward.

In short, for gardeners in countries with well-marked seasons much of the satisfaction comes from working with the climate in addition to that inevitable feeling of one-upmanship of having brought forward or extended the period of which one is most fond by either cultivational guile or plain expertise.

Vegetables

While the all-year-round garden refers particularly to effects from flowering plants, which is a relatively new concept in gardening, the vegtables and fruit are not to be neglected in this context and earlier chapters on those topics attempt to make that point. It is always worth studying the recommendations (though perhaps with just a small pinch of salt) of the seed catalogues. New varieties are continually being bred for earliness, hardiness, flavour and so on and it is a mistake to stick to the old favourites too religiously. Sometimes a vegetable entirely new to our gardens appears as with Chinese cabbage for an admirable autumn salad or sugarloaf chicory for use well into the New Year. While once we had to rely on lettuce and the vagaries of the weather, salads are now available from the outdoor unprotected garden throughout the year.

Protected Places

It is, then, a combination of factors which take us from the fireside and television into the garden during the winter weekends. And one of the most important aspects is its basic design. Emphasis has already been put on the importance of a spot to catch the first or last of the warm sun, quiet and out of the wind. This may be usable for morning coffee or even lunch as late as the end of October and as soon as early March. Quick drying paving or wooden decking is vital here: sun on the face is little compensation for shoes soaking up the wet.

Winter-Flowering Plants

In such places the winter-flowering plants are necessary. *Mahonia japonica* will give scented sprays of yellow flowers from November to April inclusive and look splendidly statuesque for the rest of the year. Chimonanthus, the winter sweet, though taking up to ten years to settle down to flower well, is worth waiting for: a couple of sprigs of its horn-yellow bells will scent its area or a whole room. (It is a dull plant in summer but makes a useful support for a clematis, this is a way of getting two for the price of one.) Winter cherry bursts out into flower every time there is a mild spell, and there are numbers of other woody plants to give interest at this time.

At a lower level, no garden should be without *Iris unguicularis* (the Algerian or stylosa iris). It is ideally suited to be left alone in a narrow border against the house, even in a gravel path, in the hottest position available to provide some of the most ethereally beautiful flowers for cutting throughout the winter. You may be lucky with Christmas roses (*Helleborus niger*) but they won't flower well for everyone. However, other hellebores, notably *H. orientalis*, *H. atrorubens* and *H. corsicus*, most certainly will if rather later. They all mix well at the base of shrubs and enjoy the summer shade.

Early flowering bulbs are usually small enough to fit into the tiniest courtyard garden. What is desirable is that, in most cases, they should be left alone. A few aconites or snowdrops could surround a tree set

in the lawn placed really close to the trunk so that the leaves which must be allowed to die down naturally in late spring, are not a bother. Various wild crocus species start to open in February. *Crocus tomasinianus* is a delicate lavender and is happy under deciduous shrubs, *C. chrysanthus* and all its lovely forms are not much later. These are admirable in a raised bed or against the edges of paving. There is certainly no lack of delightful flowering plants to link autumn to spring and tempt the gardener out.

Other Attractions

Other aspects include shrubs with coloured bark and ornamental berries. (Remember that in areas with a voracious bird population yellow berries last longer than red, no doubt they think such fruits are still unripe). And, of course, the clothed or furnished look that

The all-year-round garden is bound to mean interest from flowering plants, with fruit and vegetables from the kitchen garden throughout the twelve months of the year. Even in a cool temperate climate this is not an impossible ideal. But it also means a dry paved area with chairs and table from which to enjoy the fruits of one's labour.

carefully chosen evergreens give is invaluable. No winter garden can be inviting if everything is leafless and apparently dead. Obviously, especially in small gardens, heavy evergreen shade is quite unacceptable. Avoiding this, however, there are small conifers available in every shade of green, to near blue and gold; broad-leaved evergreens also exist in striking variegated forms. *Elaeagnus pungens* 'Maculata' is as bright as a forsythia bush in full

bloom, especially when caught by the low winter sun. All of these provide invaluable cut material for indoors.

Dry walks should lead to most if not all of these plants – another reason for edging lawns with paving. And, similarly, it should also be possible to reach any rows of winter vegetables dry-shod. The rows themselves should be short in order to reduce traffic on the wet soil, not only for convenience but to avoid puddling down the ground. On a heavy clay it is wise to have a few planks to lay alongside rows which need frequent visiting. But even here change is apparent. New varieties of Brussels sprouts have helped the problem as the sprouts develop nearly simultaneously up the stem; this can be cut whole and the picking done at leisure indoors – another reason for finding new varieties for new needs.

However lovely a plant may be in its season of floral beauty it does not earn its place in the all-year-round garden unless it has other attributes as well.

Left Other emphases for long season interest come from leaves. The range of greens, greys, gold, variegated and purple combine to offer endless interest. This border has variegated Hosta undulata, Sedum sieboldii *and the sulphur-yellow flowers of* Alchemilla mollis *backed by the foliage of* Helleborus foetidus. *The strong foliage of bergenia dominates the grouping with the grey leaves of* Stachys lanata *in the background.*

Below The corkscrew hazel is one, however, which does. Throughout the winter especially if it can be planted in a somewhat raised position the twisted branches, each looking as if it grew entirely for the benefit of some specialist in ikebana, stand out against the light. When the catkins come it is transformed into a different creature for weeks together.

House and Garden

MUCH OF THIS BOOK HAS BEEN concerned with the linking of house and garden, suggesting that the rigid demarcation between them is both unnecessary and a bar to contemporary living – even when the contemporary living is in an old house. The point has been made more than once that although much garden furniture, collapsible or wicker soft-seated chairs, has to be taken indoors after use in all but the most settled weather, it is desirable to arrange for permanent seats in one of two places. It is not always convenient to get a garden chair out; so often 'I've only a moment' and morning coffee is taken on the edge of the kitchen table littered with earlier debris. A bench by the kitchen door entices outside and the garden has another link with the daily life of the house. Wherever a niche or alcove can be contrived a seat can be considered, by vegetable plot (and especially allotment) and flower bed alike. It always seems a major misfortune that people are heard to say, not without a certain smug self-righteousness, that they are far too busy actually gardening to ever have time to sit in their garden. If this is the case it seems that motives need a certain examination.

We garden, then, because we like to embellish our home; because we like plants; because home-produced fruit and vegetables usually taste better than those for sale in shops; because they help towards the basic economics of living; because the exercise is enjoyable and combines with a certain atavistic feeling that is the personal connection with the life-giving earth; pantheism indeed.

The obverse of this same coin, garden and house; consider the encouraged intrusion of plants into areas designed and built for people. The number of people who run greenhouses is proportionally small but there must be few households who do not use a window ledge for a plant or two. An ideal greenhouse is a controlled environment for the successful growing of plants; a dwelling house is, if Le Corbusier be believed, a machine for living in which ameliorates local climate and conditions for the benefit of human inhabitants. Paradoxically what most humanises and softens our house interiors is plant growth.

It is suitable, therefore, that our houses, sheds, as well as custom-built greenhouses, can be used to grow plants which could not survive the normal climate outdoors. Many of these should be considered as bridging the house and garden divide to link one with the other.

Conventional terms are apt to be confusing or at least restricting; 'house plants' are apt to refer to truly tropical, forest-floor plants which are evolutionarily adapted to the low light levels also experienced indoors. (It is apt to be forgotten that light is essential as an energy source in plant metabolism.) So long as temperatures are adequate many plants in this group will survive

Three fine plants for house and garden embellishment:

Left *The lovely white angel's trumpet* (Datura suaveolens) *is a tropical plant but one which if kept nearly dry in its pot will overwinter happily at temperatures around 4.5°C (40°F) to be stood out in summer where its evening scent can be enjoyed.*

Right *Forsythia is an utterly hardy shrub which can be used the other way round, Bring it indoors in January to brighten the dullest of months.*

Below *Winter flowering bulbs are always a joy but the range goes beyond what flowers naturally a little later outside. Here is lachanalia from South Africa, waxy and surprisingly long-lasting.*

without much complaint. Infinitely better, both for the plants and their civilising effect in the house, is to group a number of complementary species in some form of jardinière: this rather grandiloquent word can include anything from ormolu to lead, from footbath to plastic

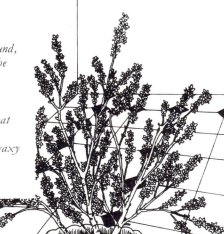

bucket. What is important is the luxuriance of foliage which makes each species mutually advantageous to its fellows. Recent advances in hydroculture make such houseplant groups virtually foolproof. But they are not, with very few exceptions, flowering plants.

For these a clearer house and garden juxtaposition comes into sight. Typical are the myriads of bulbs planted in pots and bowls each autumn throughout the land. Sadly the bulbs and their producers come in for a lot of abuse as hyacinths open flowers at the base of 45-cm (18-in) high leaves or when daffodils abort completely. Such abuse is usually unjustified, failure being the result of bad cultivation. The open garden should be enjoined to help. Except for those bulbs described as 'prepared' in which refrigeration and heat treatment have artificially broken down the normal dormancy pattern, all need a relatively long period for root development before being encouraged to begin shoot growth. There is no better way of making sure the growth pattern occurs in the right order than plunging the pots (though not containers without drainage holes) in a pile of coarse sand or weathered ashes in a shady spot in the open, however cold. Occasional examination will show when a couple of inches of top growth is supported by a pot full of roots.

With heated greenhouse help there is no lack of fine plants which, season by season, can enliven rooms indoors. A cold greenhouse or lean-to conservatory is apt to be neglected for this, it being generally considered suitable only for summer crops of tomatoes and so on. Nothing could be further from the truth.

Winter temperatures, in all but the coldest areas, are sufficiently ameliorated to make numbers of nearly or entirely hardy plants suitable for house use. A few wall-flowers and Brompton stocks

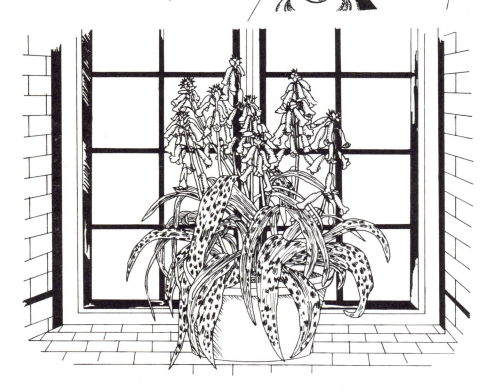

can be potted up in September; polyanthus are equally good. Small alpine bulbs which flower so early outside that their blooms are apt to get spoilt are a revelation. Their scent at nose level is frequently amazing: a treatise could be written about the range of perfumes given out by dwarf irises alone. And after a first season so grown they can be planted outdoors to bulk up the garden scene in the future (only *Iris danfordiae*, that exquisite early yellow subject seems incapable of building up flowering bulbs again). Tender bulbs such as lachenalias and veltheimia should also be tried.

On a larger scale, but not beyond the resources of a small garden, is to grow a half dozen early flowering shrubs in pots plunged by the garden shed or in the vegetable garden – *Viburnum × burkwoodii*, *Forsythia ovata*, *Deutzia gracilis*, even a small laburnum. These only need an occasional feed to build up flower buds. They are then brought into the house in late winter and burst into what seems the most exotic flower. Often this sort of pattern occurs in the opposite direction: a small flowering shrub is bought for the house, an azalea perhaps or the exquisite *Cytisus racemosus*. After flowering it sits outside the back door until it dies of drought and neglect. Immediate plunging in a sheltered spot after flowering would prevent this (so long as frosts are over, for it must be remembered that a period indoors has probably brought on unseasonably soft foliage and if this is damaged next year's flower potential is ruined). In the case of azaleas their need for lime-free water must be remembered: if gardening on a limy soil a few small rhododendrons or camellias grown for the house in this manner is one way of breaking the calcifuge barrier.

A further house and garden liaison comes when using the protection of the former to supply tender exotics for standing out on the terrace in summer. There is no doubt that a tub of agapanthus, a fine fuchsia or two and possibly the splendid angel's trumpet, *Datura suaveolens*, adds a touch of luxury to summer sitting out. Traditionally these plants overwinter under glass, in less opulent situations a light shed or an unheated spare bedroom manages surprisingly well. Water should be withheld gradually from the plants in late autumn and they are brought undercover when hard frost threatens – a degree or two does little harm and if they can stay out until the end of November all the better. Woody shoots are reduced in length. They are kept barely moist and in a state of suspended animation from which they are awakened by gentle spraying with water at the end of March.

This interaction between house and garden helps to maintain plant interest in both places: other examples will be thought of as individual requirements and enthusiasms come to the fore. The general emphasis is on the fact that neither place should be entirely type-cast. That way lies conventionality and boredom.

House and garden perfectly integrated with the division of great sliding glass doors being barely perceptible. Carpet gives way to paving, and paving to plants on both sides of the doors. Only the weather is going to restrict full use of the whole picture. Such a garden is remarkably little trouble, very seldom is any major effort required. What is needed, however, is continual observation and interest to give the care that encourages the clematis to climb the right way, and the annuals to continue to flower, as well as to be relentless in replacing the mediocre with the best that is available.

Acknowledgments

Garden plans by Allan Hart AILA AIPRA
Colour artwork by Chris Forsey
Line artwork by Norman Barber, David Bryant, Peter Crump, Sue Finch and Ingrid Jacobs

The Author would like to thank Barbara Haynes, Susanne Mitchell and Gail Rose of The Hamlyn Group for their help and support in the preparation of this book.

The publishers would like to thank Mrs. Stanley Wise for the use of her garden for photographic purposes and Machin Designs Ltd. for providing some artwork reference.

Thanks are also due to Brecht-Einzig Ltd., Pat Brindley, The Daily Telegraph, Hamlyn Group Picture Library – Sally Chappell, David Johnson, Tania Midgley, Allen Paterson, Robert Pearson, The Harry Smith Photographic Collection, David Stevens and Michael Warren for colour photographs.

Bibliography

Useful further reading:

A. *General*
The Collingridge Illustrated Encyclopaedia of Gardening by A. G. L. Hellyer
The Reader's Digest Encyclopaedia of Garden Plants
A Gardener's Dictionary of Plant Names by A. W. Smith and W. T. Stearn

B. *Specific*
Hilliers' Manual of Trees and Shrubs
Perennial Garden Plants by G. S. Thomas

Plants for Ground Cover by G. S. Thomas
Shrubs for the Milder Counties by W. Arnold-Forster
Gardening on Chalk and Limestone by E. Bertram Anderson
Gardening in the North by K. Lemmon
The Fruit Garden Displayed A Royal Horticultural Society Publication
The Vegetable Garden Displayed A Royal Horticultural Society Publication

Index

Figures in bold refer to photographs or illustrations

Acanthus **54**
access 118
Acer palmatum dissectum **92**
Aconite 145
Actinidia chinensis 142
Agapanthus 150
air: importance of 14
Alchemilla mollis **146**
all-year-round garden 144–7
alpines 127
Alstroemeria **54**
Androsace 103
Angelica 65–7
annuals 57
    in containers 25
    in shade 41
aphids 50
Apple trees: training **140**, 141, **142–3**
arches 17
Artemisia
    arborescens **54**
    'Lambrook Silver' 17, 68
Artichoke
    Globe **136**, 139
    Jerusalem 57
Arundinaria murieliae 95
Asparagus 57, 139
Asparagus Pea 61
Aubergine 127, 137, 139
Aubrieta 103
Aucuba 40
Auricula 29
Azalea 12, **115**, 127, 150

Bamboo 95
Banana 36
barbecue **129**
Basil **64**, 65
Bay trees **116**
Beans, Runner 25, 137
bedding plants 57
beds, raised **49**, **50–1**
    for disabled 50
    herbs in 65
    for rock plants 103–4, **104**
    shrubs for 40
Belloc, Hilaire 133

Berberis 29
    darwinii 52
Bergenia 41, **146**
bird baths 133
bird table 29
birds 29
Blackberries 142
Blackcurrants 142
Bluebell, Spanish 57
Borage 65
borders 16–17
botanical nomenclature 53–5
Brassicas 29
Broom 61, 103
Brown, Capability 12, 15, 88
Brussels Sprouts 137, 147
Buddleia
    fallowiana alba 31
    f. 'Lochinch' 31
buildings, garden 120–2
bulbs 127
    alpine 150
    early-flowering 145
    in pots 149
    in shade 40–1
Busy Lizzie 41, **41**
butterflies 28, 29–31

Cabbage 20, 137
calcifuge plants 20
Caltha palustris plena **53**
Camellia 20, 24, 40, 52, 115, 150
    x williamsii 24
Campanula **103**
carbon dioxide enrichment 14
car parking 118
Carrots **137**, 139
Cauliflower 137, **137**
Cercidiphyllum **61**
    japonicum 61
Cestrum parqui 129
chalk: soil found on 20
chalky soil 14
Chamomile 110
character 12–13
Cherry 52
    flowering 118
    sweet 140

children:
    danger of pools to 95, 97
    gardening for 47
    garden for 44–7, **46–7**
Chimonanthus 145
Chinese Gooseberries 142
Chives **64**
Christmas Rose 145
Chrysanthemum coronarium 61
Cineraria 127
Cistus 17, 42, **119**, 129
Citrus 127
clay soil 13, 14, 20
    water retention 14
Clematis 145
climate 20–1
    importance of 13
    judging from plants 72
    map of Europe **21**
climbers 24–5, 69
    supporting 25, **25**
climbing frame **44**
coal bunker, screening 122
cold: plants tolerant of 115
Columbine **118**
compost heap 17, 25
composts:
    for containers 113
    John Innes 113
conifers: dwarf 103, 127
conservatory **126–7**
containers 112–15, **112**, **113**, **114**, **115**
    care of plants in 115
    compost for 113
    plants for 113–15
    rock plants in 103–4
    selection 112–13
    shrubs in 40
Coriander 65
Corylus avellana contorta
    (Corkscrew Hazel) 95, **147**
Cotoneaster 29, 52, 103
    horizontalis **52**
    lacteus 38
    microphyllus 34, 109
    salicifolia 'Repens' 109
Cotula 110
country gardens 28, 30–1
    for non-gardeners 59